Hilary Synnott

The Causes and Consequences of South Asia's Nuclear Tests

Adelphi Paper 332

Oxford University Press, Great Clarendon Street, Oxford OX2 6DP
Oxford New York
Athens Auckland Bangkok Bombay Calcutta Cape Town
Dar es Salaam Delhi Florence Hong Kong Istanbul Karachi
Kuala Lumpur Madras Madrid Melbourne Mexico City
Nairobi Paris Singapore Taipei Tokyo Toronto
and associated companies in
Berlin Ibadan

Oxford is a trade mark of Oxford University Press

Published in the United States
by Oxford University Press Inc., New York

© The International Institute for Strategic Studies 1999

First published December 1999 by **Oxford University Press** for
The International Institute for Strategic Studies
23 Tavistock Street, London WC2E 7NQ

Director John Chipman
Editor Gerald Segal
Assistant Editor Matthew Foley
Project Manager, Design and Production Mark Taylor

British Library Cataloguing in Publication Data
Data available

Library of Congress Cataloguing in Publication Data

ISBN 0-19-929001-6
ISSN 0567-932X

contents

glossary

AEC	Atomic Energy Commission (India)
AIADMK	All India Anna Dravida Munnetra Kazhagam (India)
ARF	ASEAN Regional Forum
ASEAN	Association of South-East Asian Nations
ASEM	Asia–Europe Meeting
BJP	Bharatiya Janata Party (India)
CTBT	Comprehensive Nuclear Test Ban Treaty
DAE	Department of Atomic Energy (India)
DRDO	Defence Research and Development Organisation (India)
G-8	Group of Eight industrial nations
GDP	gross domestic product
IAEA	International Atomic Energy Agency
ICBM	intercontinental ballistic missile
IDSA	Institute for Defence Studies and Analyses (India)
IMF	International Monetary Fund
MEA	Ministry of External Affairs (India)
MQM	Mohajir Qaumi Mahaz
MTCR	Missile Technology Control Regime
NAM	Non-Aligned Movement
NPT	Nuclear Non-Proliferation Treaty

NRDC	Natural Resources Defense Council (US)
NSAB	National Security Advisory Board (India)
NSG	Nuclear Suppliers' Group
PAL	Permissive Action Link
PML	Pakistan Muslim League
SAARC	South Asia Association for Regional Cooperation
UNMOGIP	UN Military Observer Group in India and Pakistan
WMD	weapons of mass destruction

introduction

The nuclear tests conducted by India and Pakistan in May 1998 shook the region and challenged the near-global consensus on non-proliferation. Just a year after staking their claims to nuclear status, the two countries were embroiled in a bloody clash over Kashmir, coming close to their fourth major conflict since independence. Nowhere else in the world is there a confrontation between two nuclear powers as volatile as that in South Asia. The international community has been largely powerless in its response, and its warnings and proposals have had little impact. How justified is the fear that nuclear weapons will be used to settle a territorial dispute two generations old? Could the world now be facing a nuclear flash-point in a Kashmiri mountain village? Strategic and territorial tensions have long bedevilled relations between India, Pakistan and China. In the wake of the tests, the region's underlying problems have become still more intractable, while the need to resolve them has grown more urgent than ever.

Attempts to deal with the consequences of the tests are inseparable from the history of nuclear developments in both India and Pakistan. The timing of India's tests was determined by the pro-nuclear stance of the Bharatiya Janata Party (BJP), which led the country's coalition government. But other factors – political, scientific and military pressure; the region's history of conflict; anxiety about China; a quest for international prestige; and arms-control developments – were also important. Pakistan's decision to follow India's tests with ones of its own was informed by long-held concerns about its strategic vulnerability in any conflict with India; by pressures from its scientific community; by the need to forestall any Indian attempts at regional domination; and also for reasons of self-esteem.

The tests provoked an international outcry. India and Pakistan needed to pay a price for their actions, regional stability needed to be restored, and other countries deterred from emulating their example. But outside governments were ill-equipped to deal with the new situation, and the root causes of the subcontinent's problems were beyond their powers to resolve. Sanctions were ineffective, and certainly did not cause the public in either India or Pakistan to repudiate the actions of their governments. In the year following the tests, alarm and outrage subsided, sanctions were eased, and stalled aid programmes restarted. Contacts between China and India resumed. Far from feeling chastised or ostracised, both New Delhi and Islamabad marked the first anniversary of their tests with national celebrations.

These were, however, unjustified and premature. The confrontation in Kashmir in 1999 cast doubt on claims that nuclear weapons would help to prevent war. If they led to complacency about regional stability, nuclear weapons could in fact encourage low-level conflict, with the attendant risks of escalation. Neither India nor Pakistan has revealed much about their nuclear doctrines or intentions, about the nature and disposition of weapons, or about how they will be controlled. There have been few signs of concrete steps to safeguard against accidents, unauthorised use or faulty assessments of others' intentions. Far from furthering the two countries' apparent objectives, the tests have in fact set them back. International condemnation damaged India's status and image, undermining its attempts to secure permanent membership of the UN Security Council. Relations between India and Pakistan, and between India and China, worsened, and the economic costs were high, especially for Pakistan. Despite the domestic popularity of the tests, they did little to improve the position of India's BJP-led government, which fell within a year. Similarly, the BJP's return to power in October 1999 owed little to the country's claim to nuclear status. Pakistan's adventurism in Kashmir raised fresh doubts about its leadership, which was toppled in a military coup shortly afterwards.

There are deep contradictions between international demands on India and Pakistan and the situation as it currently stands. Third-party involvement risks making matters worse, rather than better, and there can be no 'quick-fix'. The international community faces two related dilemmas:

- inducing India and Pakistan to cooperate in non-proliferation efforts without legitimising their possession of nuclear weapons and further undermining existing non-proliferation agreements; and
- reducing the risks surrounding nuclear weapons without assisting in their development.

This paper explores what should be done to mitigate the potentially dangerous effects of the presence of nuclear weapons on the subcontinent. It examines the reasons why India chose to test, and why Pakistan followed suit; assesses the international reaction, the impact on regional relations and the prospects for progress towards stability; and evaluates the development of India and Pakistan's nuclear capabilities and doctrines. The nuclear dangers on the subcontinent have been apparent for many years. What is needed now is a new approach to deal with them.

chapter 1

Why Test in 1998?

India's nuclear tests on 11 and 13 May 1998 caught the world
unawares. While there were many reasons for dismay, there was
little cause for surprise. The possibility that India would officially
declare that it possessed nuclear weapons, and would test them, had
existed at least since 1974, when the country carried out its first
nuclear test. India's policy of ambiguity – of keeping its options open
– was born even earlier, with New Delhi's decision in the late 1960s
not to accede to the Nuclear Non-Proliferation Treaty (NPT).[1]
Arguments in favour of overt nuclear status had in particular
increased since 1995, as pressure grew to conclude and then sign the
Comprehensive Nuclear Test Ban Treaty (CTBT) and nuclear-capable
missiles became ready for deployment; colourful parallels were even
drawn between nuclear weapons and the *Brahmastra*, the mythical
weapon of Brahma, the Creator of the Hindu Trinity.[2] But there were
also powerful arguments against changing the policy of ambiguity.
Doing so would break with the Gandhian and Nehruvian pacifist
tradition, would attract an adverse international reaction and would
have direct and indirect economic costs. These arguments – together
with some brazen disinformation and what the US Congressional
Research Service has described as 'the tendency of analysts to
discount seemingly irrational initiatives by other countries' –
contributed to the international surprise that greeted the 1998 tests.[3]

Pakistan had adopted a similar policy of ambiguity at around
the same time as India. Unofficial statements vaunting the country's

nuclear capabilities had been made under successive governments and, once out of office, former prime ministers had dropped strong hints that Islamabad possessed nuclear weapons. These were always formally denied. Both India and Pakistan were nonetheless widely believed either to have nuclear weapons, or to be able to produce them quickly. Along with Israel, both countries were described as 'threshold nuclear states', with a deterrence variously dubbed 'existential', 'virtual', 'opaque', 'recessed' or 'phantom'.[4] Crises in 1987 and 1990 sorely tried the policy of ambiguity in both India and Pakistan, and in 1995 India came close to declaring nuclear-weapon status. Nonetheless, New Delhi's policy did not change, and Islamabad was not prepared to act alone. Why then did the BJP, so soon after taking office in March 1998, choose to test, thereby abandoning India's long-standing position? And why did Pakistan follow suit?

Indian Motivations

The international debate which preceded the tests revolved around three main options:

- first, renouncing the option of possessing nuclear weapons by adhering to the NPT;
- second, maintaining an 'existential deterrent' (in practice, a slightly modified version of the status quo), which provided a degree of military security, without entailing high risks or significant international disapproval; or
- third, establishing an overt nuclear capability and an effective and credible deterrent.

The US and other Western countries favoured the first option; the second represented conventional political wisdom in India; while the third was advocated by a well-established, organised and vocal section of India's political and military community, as well as by some Western academics.

When India declared itself a nuclear power, it became the first country to do so since China in 1964. For secrecy's sake, the decision involved only a small group of people, with the ultimate responsibility resting with Prime Minister Atal Bihari Vajpayee. There was no prior consultation with the BJP's many coalition partners, and the armed forces, traditionally distant from the formulation of high strategy, were almost certainly not consulted. Professor William Walker has aptly described the tests as 'a lashing out – against Pakistan, against China, against the nuclear weapons states, against the non-proliferation regime'.[5] India's motivations were many and complex. They include long-standing security concerns, and the country's deep rivalry with China, with attendant worries about the possible direction of Beijing's own nuclear development. Testing was attractive to the BJP as a way of emphasising its identity, while the quickening momentum of technological development was making the need to evaluate the country's capabilities increasingly urgent. Finally, questions of Indian prestige seemed to be at stake: nuclear weapons had long been seen in some quarters in India as indicators of state power. As the consensus on non-proliferation widened in the 1990s, India's ambiguous policy towards its nuclear capability came under increasing pressure.

It would be futile, and probably misleading, to single out one cause as dominant, particularly since defenders of the decision to test have themselves switched emphasis from one to another. Nonetheless, attempts to promote stability in this troubled region require some understanding of the underlying causes prompting India to abandon its long-held position.

Security and the China Factor
In his statement to parliament on 27 May 1998, Vajpayee described national security as the 'touchstone that has guided us in making the correct choice clear'.[6] This careful formulation conveys the sense of two separate decisions: to develop and refine a nuclear-weapon capability; and to make this 'clear' by declaring India a nuclear-weapon state.

The region has indeed been exceptionally troubled in the past half-century. Conflict between India and Pakistan followed their bloody partition in 1947, and broke out again in 1965 and 1971, while India and China went to war in 1962. In 1987–90, Indian forces became embroiled in the long-running hostilities in Sri Lanka. Tensions escalated between India and Pakistan in 1987, during India's *Brass Tacks* military exercise, and again in 1990, over Kashmir.[7] It is unclear whether India and Pakistan came close to using nuclear weapons in 1990, or were deterred from doing so by the recognition of each other's undeclared capabilities.[8] Although senior retired Indian and Pakistani officers have claimed that fears of nuclear use were unjustified, the situation seemed grave enough at the time for US Deputy National Security Advisor Robert Gates to visit the region in order to prevent an inadvertent escalation to war.

Leaders in New Delhi have consistently claimed that China, not Pakistan, poses the main potential threat. Pakistan's testing in April 1998 of the *Ghauri* missile, which has sufficient range to reach New Delhi, was not initially highlighted in India as a contributory factor in the decision to test. Outside observers, however, have been sceptical of Indian claims. Emphasising China and portraying Pakistan as of only marginal relevance was politically advantageous, since it placed New Delhi in the same league as Beijing and avoided the appearance of a fixation with Islamabad, despite the bitter, albeit low-intensity, conflict with Pakistan in Kashmir. Beijing had given no indication that its nuclear and missile development was being conducted with India in mind, while in the decade preceding the tests, bilateral relations had appeared to be improving.

leaders in New Delhi have consistently claimed that China, not Pakistan, poses the main potential threat

India's tests were in fact a manifestation of the country's deep-seated rivalry with China, which goes beyond questions of security *per se*. Both states see themselves as major Asian and global powers. Their political systems, strategic goals, traditions and cultures differ. The 1962 defeat had been a humiliation for India, and China's nuclear tests two years later had caused deep alarm. India claims territory in two parts of the former princely state of Jammu and Kashmir occupied by China since the 1960s, while China claims much of the north-eastern state of Arunachal Pradesh, and does not recognise Sikkim as an integral part of India. There are disagreements over the status of Bhutan and Nepal. The issue of Tibet became a major irritant in 1959, when India permitted the Dalai Lama to set up a government-in-exile on its soil, a move seen by China as interfering in its internal affairs. New Delhi's Cold War tilt towards Moscow did nothing to improve relations.

India had also become increasingly concerned about China's developing relations with Myanmar. Beijing sold arms to Yangon, established listening posts in Myanmar and gained naval visiting rights, and had also helped to improve road and communications networks in the Irrawaddy Valley. In May 1998, Indian Defence Minister George Fernandes claimed that China had trained and equipped Myanmar's army, whose strength had risen threefold.[9] In 1994, Yangon allegedly loaned the Coco Islands to China, allowing Beijing to install a listening post just 30 nautical miles from the Andamans; a naval base was also planned. In Tibet, China had allegedly lengthened air strips, making it possible for the latest Sukhoi aircraft to be stationed there. Indian commentators have also expressed concern about Beijing's development of 8,000-kilometre and 12,000km-range intercontinental ballistic missiles (ICBMs); about its possession of some 400 nuclear warheads and an armoury of nuclear artillery shells; about the potential evolution of nuclear doctrine to allow an offensive 'first strike'; and about possible Chinese nuclear coercion.[10]

China's close relationship with Pakistan in particular has been a constant source of tension. During the 1962 conflict, China officially declared its backing for Islamabad's advocacy of a plebiscite in Kashmir, which India opposed. In 1976, Pakistani President Zulfikar Ali Bhutto reached an agreement with Beijing which in India is seen as laying the foundations for cooperation in the development of nuclear weapons. In testimony before Pakistan's Supreme Court in 1977, Bhutto reportedly described the agreement as 'my greatest achievement and contribution to the survival of our people and our nation'. Periodic US sanctions on China for contravening the Missile Technology Control Regime (MTCR) have given substance to Indian concerns. In 1994, China reaffirmed its 1992 pledge to abide by the MTCR's guidelines and, in 1996, stated that it 'would not provide assistance to unsafeguarded nuclear facilities'.[11] However, in April 1996, US Secretary of Defense William Perry reported that 'China remains Pakistan's most important supplier of missile-related technologies'.[12] Three years later, the US named China as a persistent supplier of goods related to weapons of mass destruction (WMD), and stated that Chinese organisations 'continued to provide assistance to Pakistan's ballistic missile program during the first half of 1998' and that 'some assistance continues'. Examples of this help include the reported supply between 1994 and mid-1995 of ring magnets for use in Pakistan's uranium-enrichment programme at Kahuta; the supply in 1996 of equipment for a nuclear reactor under construction at Khushab; the delivery in November 1992 of 34 M-11 missiles; and assistance in building a missile plant at Fatahjung.[13] It has been suggested that Pakistan's *Shaheen* missile closely resembles China's DF-15/M-9.[14]

In a bid to manage its differences with Beijing, New Delhi decided on a policy of engagement in the late 1980s. Following tense border skirmishes at Wangdung in 1986–87, and against the background of Sino-Soviet reconciliation, Rajiv Gandhi visited China in December 1988, the first Indian prime minister to do so since Jawaharlal Nehru in 1954. In return, Chinese Prime Minister Li Peng travelled to New Delhi in 1991. Prime Minister Narasimha Rao visited Beijing two years later, when the two sides concluded an agreement on 'The Maintenance of Peace and Tranquillity along the Line of Actual Control in the China–India Border Areas', and established arrangements to take the issues forward. Bilateral trade grew rapidly, and both sides reduced their forces in border areas.

In the period before the tests, however, dissatisfaction was growing in India, and particularly within the BJP, that this policy of engagement was doing nothing to advance India's interests. Beijing appeared high-handed, even contemptuous, in its dealings with New Delhi, and India's efforts to resolve border issues were seemingly ignored. China's tendency to return military visits at a lower level upset India's sense of status, while attempts at dialogue on nuclear issues were dismissed by Beijing on the grounds that, since India was not a nuclear power, there was nothing to discuss. Finally, to Indian irritation, the West regarded China as a more important partner, despite India's democratic credentials. (This irritation preceding the tests was reflected in Indian complaints about the Western reaction after they had taken place. Indian commentators, for example, frequently contrasted the West's relatively low-key response to China's nuclear tests in 1996 with the outcry that met India's, despite New Delhi's moratorium on further testing.)

This growing sense of frustration lay behind the now-notorious statements of Indian Defence Minister Fernandes, made just before the tests. In an interview with the *Hindustan Times* on 3 May, Fernandes claimed that Chinese military and naval activities had begun to 'encircle' India along the borders with Pakistan, Myanmar and Tibet. China was India's 'potential threat number one'; discussing 'Confidence Building Measures with our immediate neighbours is not enough'.[15] In a letter to US President Bill Clinton on 11 May, leaked to the *New York Times*, Vajpayee referred to a 'deteriorating security environment, especially the nuclear environment' and stated that 'we have an overt nuclear weapon state on our borders, a state which committed armed aggression against India in 1962 ... an atmosphere of mistrust persists, mainly due to the unresolved border problem'. China had 'helped another neighbour of ours to become a covert nuclear weapons state'.[16]

Domestic Pressures

A country the size of India will always be subject to turbulence and tension, and the period surrounding the tests was no exception. Profound changes were under way within the political system. Power was shifting from the centre to the regions, and from traditional leaders to figures who had historically largely been excluded from governance. India's secular foundations were being challenged by the BJP's growing appeal.

The BJP won a plurality of seats in general elections in March 1998. Two years earlier, a BJP-led government had survived just 13 days before its many opponents cobbled together a coalition with the sole common aim of ousting it. During its brief tenure, the BJP had apparently intended to conduct nuclear tests, but was prevented from doing so by its lack of a parliamentary majority, and by its failure to win a vote of confidence.[17] Following its defeat in 1996, several developments had worked to the BJP's advantage. Its main opponent, the Congress party, had failed to restore its position following a dismal showing in the 1996 polls, and its leaders lacked either appeal or effectiveness. The emergence of Sonia Gandhi as the party's leader shortly before the 1998 elections regained some lost ground, and Congress held on to its

a country the size of India will always be subject to turbulence and tension

share of the vote. However, the collapse in support for the party's erstwhile coalition partners, the United Front and Janata Dal, meant that Congress had no chance of forming a government. India's increasingly influential and ambitious regional parties were no longer willing to set aside their own aims in order to keep the BJP from power, and instead wanted a share of government. At the same time, popular concerns about the BJP had eased. The party had widened its presence beyond its traditional heartland in India's west and Hindi-speaking north, and had governed relatively well in some states, such as Rajasthan and Delhi, while its senior leaders had cultivated a more moderate image. Through pre- and post-poll alliances with 13 other parties, the BJP secured enough seats to form India's fifth government in two years.

The price of these alliances was, however, high as each party sought its share of the spoils. Jayaram Jayalalitha, the leader of the All India Anna Dravida Munnetra Kazhagam (AIADMK) in Tamil Nadu, proved a constant threat to the coalition's stability, and the compromises necessary to retain her party's support badly damaged the government's credibility. The BJP was forced to drop several fundamental policy positions before agreement was reached on the coalition's National Agenda for Governance. These included pledges to build a temple to the Hindu god Ram at Ayodhya, where Hindu militants had razed the Babri Mosque to the ground in 1992; the abolition of Kashmir's special constitutional status; and the introduction of a Uniform Civil Code, which would have abolished separate Muslim laws governing marriage and property rights. Lack of funds and economic uncertainty made it impossible for the BJP to fulfil the ambitious promises to alleviate poverty that the party had made while in opposition. Finally, like its predecessors, the BJP's administration faced accusations of corruption. These difficulties and compromises risked alienating the BJP's supporters, who expected governance to bring progress in meeting the party's cherished objectives.

The BJP's pledge over nuclear policy was one of the few major manifesto commitments retained in the National Agenda for Governance. The pledge, which was endorsed by all coalition members, aimed to re-evaluate the country's nuclear policy and to 'exercise the option to induct nuclear weapons'. Although what 'induct' actually meant was unclear, the implication, fostered by

Indian officials, was that no change was in prospect before the promised 're-evaluation' of policy had taken place. In practice, events moved more rapidly. Given that the other key planks of its platform had been removed, nuclear testing had become increasingly important to the BJP as a way of strengthening its weak political position by assuaging disillusioned supporters and attracting new ones, without incurring significant domestic opposition.

Pressure from India's scientific community for further tests supplemented these political considerations. India's civil nuclear programme began under Nehru in 1948, when the Atomic Energy Commission (AEC) was set up. Six years later, the Department of Atomic Energy (DAE) was established with the help of, among others, the US and Canada. India's ambivalent attitude towards nuclear weapons, informed by the tradition of *ahimsa*, or non-violence, was reappraised in the wake of the country's defeat by China in 1962, and Beijing's nuclear tests two years later. Pressure to develop nuclear weapons began to grow, notably from the Bharatiya Jana Sangh, the forerunner of the BJP.[18] In 1964, Nehru's successor as prime minister, Lal Bahadur Shastri, explored the possibility of securing a nuclear guarantee from the US and the Soviet Union.[19] Following the 1965 war with Pakistan, the start of discussions on a nuclear non-proliferation treaty and vigorous debate within his Congress party, Shastri opted to concentrate on conventional forces, although he did not renounce the option to develop nuclear weapons.

The possibility of a nuclear guarantee was investigated in 1969 under Indira Gandhi, again without success, and the decision to prepare for a nuclear test was apparently taken in 1972. The move followed India's third war with Pakistan the previous year in which, as in 1965, Beijing had supported Islamabad. India was especially outraged by the arrival of the nuclear-capable *USS Enterprise* in the Bay of Bengal, which was seen as an attempt at nuclear blackmail by the US to persuade New Delhi to accept a cease-fire, and to refrain from dismembering West Pakistan.[20] Indira Gandhi's decision to proceed with the test in 1974, which was strongly influenced by unrelated domestic political factors, provoked the instant termination of foreign cooperation in India's civil nuclear programme. Policy switched three years later, when Prime Minister Moraji Desai publicly renounced testing and pledged that, under his leadership,

India would not acquire nuclear weapons. Desai's tenure was, however, brief, and the caretaker regime that followed dropped this commitment and declared that the decision to develop nuclear weapons was a sovereign Indian prerogative.

The establishment in 1983 of an Integrated Guided Missile Programme suggested that India was developing its nuclear-related capabilities further. K. Subrahmanyam subsequently claimed that he had pressed Rajiv Gandhi to exercise 'the nuclear option' when he was director of India's Institute for Defence Studies and Analyses (IDSA) in 1985. According to Subrahmanyam, India's nuclear deterrent came into existence in early 1990.[21] Technical progress in missile development sharpened the arguments. Notwithstanding the purported dual role of the *Prithvi* medium-range missile, it and the intermediate-range *Agni* only made economic and military sense if they were given a nuclear capability. As the *Prithvi* became ready for deployment in the early 1990s, so the need for greater certainty about its role and purpose increased, and political leaders came under growing pressure to test.[22]

Nuclear Weapons and Indian Prestige

India has long aspired to be in the front rank of global political powers, and has several attributes to support its bid. The country is home to over a billion people, including the world's second-largest Muslim population after Indonesia. It has a sizeable economy (ranked fifth in the world in terms of purchasing power parity), and an effective, secular constitution guaranteeing the rule of law and democratic politics. During the Cold War, the main vehicle for its global aspirations was the Non-Aligned Movement (NAM), along with an active, if sometimes idiosyncratic, role in the UN, and participation in peacekeeping operations. In 1997, India officially declared that it wished to become a Permanent Member of the UN Security Council. The year before, the country had become a full 'dialogue partner' with the Association of South-East Asian Nations (ASEAN) and a member of the ASEAN Regional Forum (ARF), to which New Delhi attached much importance. Progress in economic reform, which began in 1991, increased foreign interest in partnerships with the country, while the 'Gujral Doctrine' of 1996–97, which sought to improve relations with India's neighbours, demonstrated a new engagement with other states in South Asia.

Many Western countries backed India's bid for membership of the Asia–Europe Meeting (ASEM). India's claim to leadership seemed, however, more declaratory than real, and faced opposition from other states. During the Cold War, its NAM colleagues were reluctant to recognise its aspirations, partly because of New Delhi's relationship with Moscow, and partly because of its seemingly high-handed approach towards them. Asian countries themselves expressed doubts about India and Pakistan's membership of ASEM, both at the start of the process in 1996 and before the second ASEM summit in 1998.[23]

The view has long been held in some Indian circles, notably in the Ministry of External Affairs (MEA), that nuclear weapons are a key indicator of state power.[24] Their possession would place India on a similar level to China, and prevent nuclear blackmail by Washington or Beijing. However, the link between nuclear weapons and great-power status has weakened steadily since the end of the Cold War. The virtual consensus on future permanent membership of the Security Council for Germany and Japan rests on their economic weight, not on whether they have nuclear weapons. Other major candidates, such as Argentina, Brazil and South Africa, have renounced nuclear weapons, and won international approval by doing so. The UK and France support their continued permanent membership with their active involvement and expertise in international affairs, rather than through their nuclear capabilities, which both countries have substantially reduced. Finally, international condemnation of India's tests, and of its refusal to sign either the CTBT or the NPT, has not improved its chances of winning any vote in the UN on possible permanent membership. This lack of sympathy towards India's position over the CTBT and NPT was illustrated in 1996, when New Delhi lost its competition with Japan for non-permanent membership of the Security Council.

Developments in Arms Control

Changes in international attitudes towards nuclear weapons were reflected in progress over arms control and non-proliferation in the 1990s, which began to pose serious challenges to India's traditional posture. In 1993, India had joined the US in sponsoring a UN resolution in favour of the CTBT. By 1995, however, it had become clear that international consensus was possible, and opinion in India began to harden.[25] For India, signing a test-ban treaty without first having refined its nuclear-weapon capabilities would have formalised and perpetuated the nuclear imbalance with China. From 1996, after the indefinite extension of the NPT and a change of government in India, negotiations over the CTBT became increasingly bitter. New Delhi was particularly incensed by Article XIV, which stipulated that 44 countries including itself (all of which possessed nuclear reactors) should deposit their instruments of ratification before the treaty could enter into force. New Delhi regarded this requirement as pressure for it to sign. In 1996, India put forward amendments to emphasise the draft's discriminatory nature. The most significant was a proposal – unacceptable to the nuclear-weapon states – for a timebound framework for the total elimination of nuclear weapons. In June 1996, Arundhati Ghose, India's representative at the Conference on Disarmament in Geneva, declared that 'India cannot subscribe to [the CTBT] in its present form'.[26]

India's opposition to the NPT, which it dubbed 'nuclear apartheid', was of longer standing. For India, the NPT sanctioned 'vertical proliferation' by allowing the five existing nuclear-weapon states to modernise and improve their warheads, while preventing 'horizontal proliferation' by banning other countries from acquiring nuclear weapons. Despite Indian opposition, however, the NPT was extended indefinitely in 1995 without modification. There was little international sympathy for India's refusal to conform to this near-total consensus. The country appeared to be driven more by the desire to preserve its own room for manoeuvre than, as it had always claimed, by a quest for justice on behalf of all non-nuclear-weapon states – many of whom stood to benefit greatly from the NPT because it obviates the risk of nuclear arms races between regional neighbours.

The cross-party backlash in India against the nuclear-weapon states, the NPT and the CTBT helped to justify the argument that declaring the country's nuclear capability had become a necessity. The 'open option' – between the declaration and the renunciation of a nuclear-weapon capability – had to be closed. Indian criticism of the nuclear-weapon states for their lack of progress over nuclear disarmament was a major part of the country's justification for its tests, and for its rejection of the CTBT: since there was no agreement on the principle of a timetable for nuclear disarmament, India had no choice but to assure its security by nuclear means.

Pakistani Motivations

Pakistan claimed to have carried out five tests on 28 May, and one more two days later. Several of its reasons for testing were similar to India's. Islamabad saw India's tests as part of its bid for great-power status, and as assisting in a quest for regional domination. Pakistan has long been conscious of India's greater wealth and superior military strength and, given its lack of strategic depth, of its own vulnerability to conventional attack. Islamabad has for many years spent over 5% of its gross domestic product (GDP) on defence.

Pakistan's main focus in its relations with India has been Kashmir – the 'unfinished business of partition', according to successive governments. Despite some Indian assertions that Islamabad's interest in the area has been intermittent, and was revived in the 1990s only for opportunistic reasons, the issue has in fact dominated Pakistani foreign policy since independence.[27] Islamabad has been concerned that, if Indian domination were left unchallenged, Pakistan's claims to Kashmir would be eroded. In the years following the Simla Agreement of 1972, which stated that differences between India and Pakistan should be settled through bilateral negotiation, accommodation proved increasingly difficult. In particular, no progress was made over a secret agreement, allegedly reached at the time of the Simla Agreement, by which the Line of Control would become an international border, since this would have left the Kashmir Valley in Indian hands.[28] In an attempt to internationalise the issue, Pakistan tried to focus attention on UN resolutions of the 1940s calling for a plebiscite in Kashmir. The situation has been aggravated by human-rights abuse by Indian security forces in Kashmir and the Punjab, Indian interference in Kashmiri elections, and political and military assistance to militants in the Kashmir Valley from the Pakistani side of the Line of Control. Active confrontation continued in the Valley and in Siachen throughout the 1990s, while the Valley's population became increasingly alienated from both governments.

The dispute over Kashmir notwithstanding, the gravest difficulties facing Pakistan's government around the time of India's tests were domestic, rather than external. In elections in February

1997, Nawaz Sharif's Pakistan Muslim League (PML) won a massive majority. Sharif became prime minister, and set about removing the constitutional constraints on his power. Disputes with President Farooq Leghari, Chief Justice Sajjad Ali Shah and Chief of Army Staff General Jehangir Karamat led to the resignation or replacement of all three. Sharif acquired more powers than any elected leader since Pakistan's independence. This did not, however, result in the restoration of civil order in the country. Internal conflict continued, involving the Mohajir Qaumi Mahaz (MQM) in Karachi, Sunni–Shia sectarian violence in the Punjab and violence against minority Christian and Ahmadi religious groups elsewhere. *Taleban* excesses in Afghanistan embarrassed the government, which had supported the group; Islamic influence in North-West Frontier Province increased. In addition, the country suffered from chronic fiscal deficits, only partially mitigated by a highly developed black economy. By mid-1998, foreign debt stood at some $30bn. Foreign-currency reserves were less than $1bn (about five weeks' worth of imports), GDP growth had fallen to 3% and inflation had risen to 12%. Sharif's domestic political position was therefore significantly weaker than his party's huge parliamentary majority appeared to suggest; indeed, Pakistan's very governability seemed in doubt.[29]

> *the gravest difficulties facing Pakistan's government were domestic, rather than external*

In the days following India's tests, international pressure on Sharif not to respond in kind was intense. Although it remains unclear when the decision was taken to proceed with tests, the two-week delay allowed Sharif to present himself, unlike the Indian leadership, as sensitive to international concerns. Since India's tests would have surprised Pakistan just as much as they did the rest of the world, the interval may also have been necessary to allow time to finalise test preparations.

There were benefits to be had from restraint. Pakistan's moral standing would have been enhanced, raising the possibility of greater support for its stance on Kashmir. Conventional arms supplies would have increased, possibly including the delivery by the US of 30 F-16 aircraft, which had been embargoed since 1990 under the terms of the Pressler Amendment.[30] International financial institutions would have taken a more benign view of Pakistan's acute economic difficulties. Finally, the sanctions imposed on India would have been tougher.

Against these benefits were set seemingly compelling reasons why Pakistan should respond with tests of its own. Ultimately, the strength of domestic opinion was overwhelming. The provocative and triumphalist statements of members of the Indian leadership after the tests were taken by Islamabad, and by Pakistani public opinion, to mean that the threat from India had increased. Pakistani intelligence reports of an imminent military strike on Pakistan's nuclear facilities at Kahuta, said to be planned jointly by India and Israel, contributed to the tense atmosphere.[31] Since successive governments had declared that they would match any Indian tests, failure to do so would have undermined Sharif's already damaged credibility. The immediate international response to the Indian tests was not as tough or as punitive as Pakistan believed was warranted. Islamabad felt that Washington had not been sufficiently supportive after India's tests, thereby undermining US claims to recognise Pakistan's security concerns.

As in India, Pakistan's government faced scientific, as well as political, pressure to test the country's capabilities, and India's actions appeared to provide the opportunity to do so. Developing civil nuclear energy had not been a priority at independence, and Pakistan established an Atomic Energy Commission only in 1957. The decision to manufacture a nuclear bomb appears to have been taken in 1972.[32] Four years later, Bhutto concluded his cooperation agreement with China. By 1979, it had become clear that Pakistan had acquired uranium-enrichment technology, and the US suspended aid.[33] By 1987, the country had reportedly either acquired a nuclear-weapon capability, or had come close to doing so. With the Soviet withdrawal from Afghanistan, Pakistan's importance as a front-line Cold War state diminished, and US scrutiny of its nuclear activities increased. In 1990, US President George Bush was unable to certify that Pakistan did not possess a nuclear explosive device, and further sanctions were imposed. Like India, Pakistan was also developing missile systems. However, whereas India's *Agni* was of relevance primarily to China, Pakistan's missile development, reportedly helped by both China and North Korea, was conducted exclusively with India in mind. The 600km-range *Hatf* III was tested in mid-1997, and the 1,500km *Hatf* V, also known as the *Ghauri*, was test-fired on 6 April 1998, shortly before India's tests.

India's nuclear tests took place amid growing political and strategic pressure on the leadership to declare that the country was a nuclear-weapon state. The government explained its decision primarily in terms of a threat from China, and as a result of insufficient progress towards global nuclear disarmament. But considerations of prestige and concerns about the extent of Pakistan's capabilities also played a role, together with advice from the scientific community that delivery systems were approaching readiness, and that tests were needed. Given the BJP's previous policy statements, and the compromises that it had to make over its election manifesto, the timing of the decision, if not its nature, must have been influenced by the need for domestic political advantage. Having taken its decision, the Indian government appeared to overplay the imminence of any threat posed by China, and the extent to which India's security would be enhanced, rather than diminished, by declaring the country's nuclear-weapon capability. Unnecessary and provocative criticism of China, bellicose remarks about Kashmir and a seeming disregard for international opinion provoked widespread criticism.

chapter 2

After the Tests

International Reactions

The Indian and Pakistani tests prompted immediate condemnation; 152 individual states, together with a stream of international organisations – the Group of Eight (G-8) industrial nations, the European Union, the Organisation of American States, the Gulf Cooperation Council, the Organisation of the Islamic Conference and the Nordic Council of Ministers – all voiced their opposition. In July, the ARF issued a critical communiqué that was unprecedented in that it was adopted without consensus.[1] NAM members expressed their dismay at the organisation's summit in South Africa the following September.[2]

The most influential forum in coordinating the immediate international response to the tests was a special meeting of foreign ministers from the five Permanent Members of the UN Security Council, which was held on 4 June under Chinese chairmanship. The benchmarks set out in the communiqué which followed the meeting were reflected in UN Security Council Resolution 1172, adopted on 6 June, which demanded that India and Pakistan refrain from further nuclear tests. It set out a series of guidelines intended to restore stability, and to bring the two countries into the mainstream of the non-proliferation regime. The resolution, the most significant and most formal expression of international condemnation, urged New Delhi and Islamabad to resume their stalled dialogue, specifically mentioning Kashmir as one of the root causes of the tensions between them. Both countries were also enjoined immediately to stop their development of nuclear weapons; to cease the production of fissile material for nuclear weapons and to participate in negotiations for a treaty banning such production; to refrain from weaponising or deploying nuclear weapons; and to become parties to the NPT and the CTBT. The resolution explicitly ruled out recognition of India and Pakistan's claims to be nuclear-weapon states, since to do so would have been incompatible with the NPT. On 11 and 12 June, unprecedented meetings were held in London. The G-8 nations were joined by China, the ambassadors or foreign ministers of Argentina, Brazil, South Africa and Ukraine (all of which had voluntarily renounced nuclear weapons) and a representative from the Philippines, acting on behalf of ASEAN. These meetings established a Task Force of senior officials from a still-wider range of countries to coordinate the international community's general expressions of concern. The group met twice in 1998, and a further three times in 1999.

This near-universal dismay, expressed by both developed and developing states, appeared to take the Indian government by surprise. Had New Delhi followed its tests with specific undertakings to come closer to international norms, such as signing the CTBT, the immediate response may have been less sharp. But its cautious, conditional and ill-defined references to a voluntary moratorium on testing and to minimal deterrence did not impress, and suggested that Indian decision-makers either had not given much thought to how to assuage international concern, or did not much care.

had New Delhi followed its tests with specific undertakings, the immediate response may have been less sharp

Sanctions

Some 14 countries adopted concrete measures to underscore their concern. The most far-reaching were taken by the US, which on 16 June announced a range of sanctions, as it was legally required to do under the Glenn Amendment to the Arms Export Control Act. These included:

• halting development aid, except for humanitarian purposes;

- suspending sales and deliveries of military equipment;
- stopping new commitments of credits and credit guarantees by government bodies;
- seeking other countries' support for postponing loans by international financial institutions;
- prohibiting US banks from extending loans or credits to government entities in India and Pakistan; and
- toughening controls on exports of dual-use equipment.[3]

Japan, which had long linked its aid programme to non-proliferation issues, also responded swiftly, halting any new aid from its large programmes to both countries.[4] (In 1997, Tokyo had offered nearly $1bn of loans and $26m in grants to India, and loans of $230m, together with grants of $41m, to Pakistan.) Other countries also cut or froze aid programmes. However, only the sanctions imposed by the US and Japan were of material significance. While no developing country went beyond declarations of condemnation or regret, neither was there significant opposition to sanctions in principle. The issue of trade sanctions did not arise, and none was imposed.

The arguments in favour of sanctions were not publicly aired in any detail by those governments that favoured them. The rationales customarily given for sanctions include:

- punishing violations of 'global norms' (although in this case the tests did not contravene any international treaty commitment);
- coercing their targets into falling back into line, or at least exercising restraint;
- expressing disapprobation;
- deterring other states; and
- meeting domestic expectations of a firm response.

Even if they could not turn the clock back, it could be argued that sanctions would at least show that there was a price to be paid for actions which the international community had made clear would have unwelcome consequences. Blameless individuals may suffer but, if sanctions were tough enough, they might prompt electors to bring their government to account.

But sanctions also raised serious dilemmas, both in practice and in principle. The key questions were whether agreement on meaningful measures could be achieved and, if so, whether these measures would have the intended effect. On both counts, the prospects were not good. The unusual international consensus condemning the tests contrasted with the widely differing views about the principle, appropriateness and effectiveness of 'punitive' measures. Russia voiced its opposition to sanctions the day after the first Indian test, arguing that New Delhi's unwelcome policy should be changed through diplomacy, not coercion. The French position was similar, putting paid to any general adoption of a sanctions package. Consensus on a UN sanctions regime, on the grounds that the nuclear tests constituted a threat to peace and security, was out of the question. Russia, France and China quickly made clear that their defence sales – and, in the case of Russia, civil nuclear cooperation – would continue.[5] Opinion was also divided within the G-8. The group's decision to 'work for a postponement in consideration of other loans in the World Bank' but not to 'oppose loans by [international financial institutions] to the two countries to meet basic human needs' was the only concrete measure on which all eight members could agree. The formulation was a compromise between, on the one hand, the United States' domestic legal obligations and the widely shared wish to express concrete disapproval and, on the other, the desire to avoid ineffective or counter-productive 'punishment'. The decision was nonetheless significant: voting arrangements in the World Bank would not have allowed the US to hold back World Bank loans without the support of other states. To obtain this backing, the explicit exemption in the case of 'basic human needs' was essential.

It was also unclear whether sanctions would have a salutary effect on other countries, where economic and political conditions were very different. In India and Pakistan, they seemed likely to bolster support for the tests, and harden opposition to external coercion. Economic sanctions would, by definition, increase India's isolation, undoing international efforts to support and encourage the outward-looking reforms that Narasimha Rao and his finance minister, Manmohan Singh, had so effectively begun in 1991. In the complex domestic environment surrounding the tests, a return to the politically resonant *swadeshi* policy of self-reliance seemed a distinct possibility. There were also moral difficulties. Although cutting development assistance would have responded to taxpayers' expectations ('if they can afford bombs, they don't need aid'), doing so would have primarily affected people with no influence over decisions on nuclear policy. The UK's programmes to India and Pakistan – its largest and third-largest respectively – focused on alleviating poverty, and remained largely unchanged. Bilateral aid programmes accounted for only a tiny proportion of India's gross national product in any case, and offered no effective political leverage.

Since it was well-known that both India and Pakistan had long possessed a nuclear capability in all but name, there was no support for differentiating between the two on the grounds that India had tested first. However, economic sanctions against Pakistan, already at risk of defaulting on its $32bn of foreign debt, could have pushed the country over the edge of governability.

Given the difficulties surrounding economic sanctions, some countries instead cancelled or deferred contacts, particularly defence links, such as visits by senior officers, attendance at staff colleges, training courses and joint exercises. This military-related 'punishment' at least had the merit of appearing to fit the 'crime'. However, cutting back on dialogue and training risked reducing opportunities to influence potential decision-makers at a time when relations between India and Pakistan were becoming dangerously antagonistic. Moreover, India's military had not been involved in the decision to test, and would have been unable to secure its reversal. There was little scope for 'precision' sanctions targeting specific areas related to nuclear and missile technology. Guidelines under the MTCR and the Nuclear Suppliers' Group (NSG) sought to deny access to sensitive technology, but had in practice largely failed to do so.

The final problem with sanctions was establishing the conditions under which they could be lifted – an exit strategy. Simply linking them with the benchmarks of Resolution 1172 would not work, since it was clear that some of the requirements of the resolution could only be met over a long period. But sanctions could not remain effective indefinitely.

It rapidly became clear that sanctions, far from reversing Indian or Pakistani policy, could in fact be counter-productive by causing indiscriminate hardship and increasing obduracy in both countries. In the absence of a significant sanctions regime, the material effects on India of international disapproval were not as great as commentators or governments had previously implied.[6] Pakistan, however, suffered disproportionately, both from those sanctions that were imposed, and from the loss of confidence among external investors that led to a run on the country's currency. At bottom, pressure on India and Pakistan had historically relied on moral and ethical arguments and, in India's case, on appeals to the Gandhian tradition of pacifism, accompanied by imprecise threats. Once South Asia's nuclear genie had emerged from the bottle, no coercion would get it back.

Although concern about the tests' impact on regional stability and on arms-control regimes did not ease, sanctions were gradually relaxed, and a more pragmatic approach emerged. By mid-1998, the US had exempted agricultural exports, allowing its farmers to take part in a wheat auction in Pakistan in July. In late 1998, the US Congress adopted the India–Pakistan Relief Act (the so-called 'Brownback Amendment'). As a result of this authority, the White House in November announced that several of the measures adopted under the Glenn Amendment would be waived for one year. The US also stated that it would support the International Monetary Fund (IMF)'s negotiations with Pakistan over debt relief, including the infusion of some $1.56bn of IMF, World Bank and Asian Development Bank funds.[7] In June 1999, an addition to the Security Assistance Act extended for a further year the president's authority to waive sanctions imposed in the previous year.

This more pragmatic approach also included dialogue, and implied recognition, though not acceptance, that neither India nor Pakistan was going to accede to the NPT in the foreseeable future. US and British military-to-military contacts were reinstated in 1998. French attempts to warm relations with India, symbolised by President Jacques Chirac's visit in January 1998, continued. Senior British cabinet ministers made high-profile trips to both India and Pakistan, while the US let it be known that a visit by Clinton, which had been postponed in late 1998 for reasons ostensibly unrelated to the tests, could take place at a later date.

After several rounds of talks with both countries, the US in November 1998 outlined its five areas of emphasis:

- • encouraging early signature and ratification of the CTBT by India and Pakistan;
- • securing a halt to both countries' production of fissile material for nuclear weapons, pending conclusion of a fissile material cut-off treaty;
- • limiting the development and deployment of nuclear-capable missiles and aircraft in India and Pakistan, and encouraging other measures of strategic restraint;
- • encouraging India and Pakistan to tighten their controls on the export of sensitive materials and technology, assisted by exchanges of information and expertise; and
- • encouraging greater dialogue between India and Pakistan, and urging them both to adopt further confidence- and security-building measures.[8]

These issues – with the important exception of limiting the development of nuclear weapons – were not far away from those which the Indian government had identified, either before or shortly after the tests, as areas of possible progress. This was useful for New Delhi in countering domestic critics, who dubbed dialogue with the US 'interference' in India's affairs.

There were also signs of a more pragmatic approach from India and Pakistan, as limited progress was made on those benchmarks selected from Resolution 1172. In the months after the test, Sharif and Vajpayee agreed to take part in negotiations on a fissile material cut-off treaty, and emphasised the restraint that their countries exercised over exports of sensitive materials. At the UN General Assembly in September 1998, both prime ministers implied their willingness in principle, albeit with significant qualifications, to sign the CTBT before September 1999, when states which had ratified the treaty were due to consider how it might quickly be brought into force. Sharif set out a number of conditions, including freedom from 'coercion or pressure', the speedy removal of restrictions by international institutions, and the lifting of sanctions. He also referred to expectations of support for the resolution of the Jammu and Kashmir dispute, and parity of treatment with India.

Despite this apparently more flexible approach, efforts to broaden dialogue on Asian nuclear issues were fruitless. Although some ARF states argued that Pakistan, a non-member, should attend the forum's ministerial meeting in July 1998, no consensus was reached. A Russian proposal in December 1998 for a trilateral arrangement involving itself, China and India attracted no interest from either New Delhi or Beijing. A similar lack of enthusiasm met Russia's suggestion in April 1999 that the trilateral idea should be extended to include Pakistan.[9] Furthermore, India wanted nothing to do with the Task Force set up in June 1998.

The Impact on Regional Relations

China's immediate reaction to the first set of Indian tests was low-key. But once Vajpayee's letter of 11 May to Clinton had been made public, Beijing's tone changed markedly, and its criticism of India became unusually strong. China encouraged the firmest possible response to India's tests, and was active in every international meeting concerning them. New Delhi swiftly realised the magnitude of its diplomatic blunder, and began to repair the damage. At the ARF's ministerial meeting in Manila in July, Jaswant Singh, then Deputy Chairman of India's Planning Commission and later foreign minister, met Chinese Foreign Minister Tang Jiaxuan. In February 1999, Indian Foreign Secretary K. Ragunath visited China. The following June, Singh, hot on the heels of Pakistani Foreign Minister Sartaj Aziz, travelled to Beijing amid extensive press commentary about undoing the damage caused by Fernandes' remarks in May 1998, and assertions that relations were back on an even keel.[10] During the Kargil conflict of May–July 1999, Beijing refrained from supporting Islamabad, and referred to the importance of respecting the Line of Control, echoing the more clearly expressed concerns of other states about Pakistani involvement in the confrontation. In July, Singh declared that India would 'engage with the great powers much more purposefully and productively' than it had done before.[11]

Relations between India and Pakistan also deteriorated sharply in the wake of the tests. Exchanges of artillery fire intensified across the Line of Control, reported territorial violations increased and tensions rose. By mid-1998, however, relations had begun to improve. Vajpayee and Sharif met during a summit of the South Asia Association for Regional Cooperation (SAARC) in Sri Lanka in July 1998, and again at the UN General Assembly in September. In February 1999, Vajpayee travelled from Amritsar to Lahore in Pakistan on a newly inaugurated bus service, the first Indian prime minister ever to make a land-crossing of the border. While in Pakistan, Vajpayee underlined India's acceptance of partition by visiting the Minar-e-Pakistan, a national monument marking the site where the Muslim League had issued its first formal appeal for the creation of a separate homeland for the Muslims of British colonial India. On 21 February, the two prime ministers issued the Lahore Declaration, which included a direct reference to the 1972 Simla Agreement specifying that differences between them should be dealt with bilaterally. This served to re-emphasise India's long-standing position.[12] The declaration contained mutual undertakings to refrain from intervention and interference in each other's internal affairs and to combat terrorism. These were significant given India's frequent accusations of Pakistani intervention in the Kashmir Valley and Punjab, and Pakistani claims of skulduggery by Indian intelligence services in Karachi. A Memorandum of Understanding which accompanied the declaration set out an ambitious plan for further work, including bilateral consultation on security concepts and nuclear doctrines; advance notification of ballistic-missile tests; measures to reduce the risk of accidental or unauthorised use of nuclear weapons; conditional reaffirmation of moratoriums on nuclear tests; and reviews of communication links and confidence-building measures. At a SAARC meeting in March, Singh and Aziz agreed a timetable and procedures for talks between ministers and experts, which set out a way forward for comprehensive dialogue on bilateral issues, including Kashmir.

Two months later, however, India and Pakistan became embroiled in an unusually tense confrontation near the Kashmiri town of Kargil, on the Indian side of the Line of Control. In May, some 2,000 militants from Pakistan – described by Islamabad as *mujahideen* or 'freedom fighters' – crossed the Line of Control, occupying high ridges up to seven kilometres inside Indian territory. From there, they threatened the only road between Srinagar and Leh, and the supply-route for Indian forces on the Siachen Glacier. Militants had frequently crossed the Line over the previous decade, but this infiltration was unusually large and took place in an exceptionally inaccessible area in the north, rather than, as was customary, in the west and south.

The Indian army first detected the militants on 6 May. The government, taken by surprise, responded robustly, swiftly sending additional troops to the scene and denouncing Pakistan's presumed involvement. Air-strikes, launched on 26 May, were the first in Kashmir since the 1971 Indo-Pakistani war. Vajpayee described the infiltration as a 'violation of the Lahore Declaration and of the Simla Agreement', while Sharif warned that mounting violence could prove a 'nuclear flashpoint'.[13] New Delhi placed strict constraints on military commanders by forbidding forces to conduct air or land operations on or over the Pakistani side of the Line of Control. This constraint played well internationally. However, by the end of June the Indian government was voicing increasing concern about casualties among its forces, and about the difficulty of dislodging the intruders from such mountainous terrain without Indian forces crossing the Line – and was making this concern plain to foreign governments. International pressure on Islamabad grew and, on 4 July, Sharif and Clinton met in Washington, where agreement was reached that 'concrete steps would be taken for the restoration of the Line of Control in accordance with the Simla Agreement'. On 6 July, the Pakistani Chief of Army Staff, General Pervaiz Musharraf, stated that between 1,500 and 2,000 'Kashmiri freedom fighters' would be asked to leave their positions.[14] By the middle of the month, the conflict had subsided. Indian losses were officially put at 407 dead and 584 injured.[15] Pakistan estimated its losses at 267 killed, 204 injured and 24 missing, and claimed that India had lost 2,000 troops, with another 2,000 injured.[16] Subsequent reports suggested that India had been preparing to invade Pakistan, and referred to US satellite imagery revealing that tanks, artillery and heavy equipment were being loaded on to railway wagons; Pakistan had also begun to prepare offensive units.[17] India's MEA swiftly denied that the country had any such intention.[18]

Sharif's agreement with Clinton was much-criticised in Islamabad. Pakistani Information Minister Mushahid Husain defended his country's role in the Kargil crisis as a successful operation launched by the *mujahideen* with the full moral, political and strategic support of Pakistan. It had achieved its purpose: internationalising the Kashmir issue.[19] Pakistan's claims that it was not directly involved were not, however, accepted in Washington.[20] On 16 July, Musharraf reportedly confirmed that there was 'occasional and aggressive patrolling' by the Pakistani army on the Indian side of the Line of Control.[21] Indian Foreign Minister Singh declared on 21 July that the lesson to be drawn from the confrontation was that more resources needed to be made available to India's defence forces.[22]

The Kargil confrontation demonstrated that the absence of full-scale war between India and Pakistan since 1971 is no guarantee of continued peace. It also highlights several questions that remain unanswered in the wake of the events of May 1998. It is not clear that the possession of nuclear weapons is in itself enough to prevent full-scale war. It is, however, clear that nuclear deterrence will not prevent low-intensity conflict. The supposed nuclear balance between India and Pakistan may have encouraged some in the Pakistani leadership to expand low-level conflict in order to gain a

> *the absence of full-scale war between India and Pakistan since 1971 is no guarantee of continued peace*

military or political advantage by taking territory or by prompting third-party involvement in the dispute. By the same token, the nuclear dimension may have limited India's conventional military options in response to the infiltration. There are also questions about the degree of foreknowledge and control exercised by the Pakistani leadership, and about the effectiveness or reliability of India's intelligence capabilities. The high casualties during the crisis and accusations of Pakistani military involvement and mistreatment of prisoners could all have offered opportunities or excuses for fresh escalation. In the event, this was contained – but there can be no confidence that such will always be the case.

chapter 3

What Next?

The Kargil crisis demonstrated that international concerns about regional stability were by no means misplaced. In the year following the tests, a broad framework for handling them had been established. However, dilemmas and challenges remain which could impede progress towards meeting the benchmarks identified by the UN Security Council in June 1998.

'Nuclear-Weapon States'?

Since neither India nor Pakistan is party to the NPT or the CTBT, their tests did not contravene international law. However, Article IX of the NPT defines a nuclear-weapon state as one which 'has manufactured and exploded a nuclear weapon or other nuclear explosive device prior to 1 January 1967'. India and Pakistan's claims to this status were therefore not recognised, and Security Council Resolution 1172 explicitly ruled it out. But, despite the resolution's call for an immediate halt to India and Pakistan's nuclear-weapon programmes and for the two countries' accession to the NPT, neither is likely in the foreseeable future. Nuclear weapons exist on the subcontinent, and they and their delivery systems continue to be developed. As Jaswant Singh puts it, South Asia's nuclear weapons are 'a reality that can neither be denied, nor wished away. This category of a Nuclear Weapon State is not, in actuality, a conferment; nor is it a status for others to grant'.[1]

India has nonetheless recognised 'the well intentioned, even if somewhat misplaced, expressions of concern about nuclear stability'.[2] Fulfilling all the benchmarks set out in Resolution 1172 would clearly rectify the problem. But short of this, what can be done to mitigate the effects of the tests without appearing to legitimise them? Since coercion has not worked, can inducements be used without appearing to reward India and Pakistan for their actions? Is dialogue possible at all without breaching Article I of the NPT?[3]

This is not a new problem. In 1984, Michael Wilmshurst, then head of the British delegation to the International Atomic Energy Agency (IAEA), considered amending the NPT to create an intermediate status – between the five nuclear-weapon states and the non-nuclear-weapon states – which might 'catch' countries that would otherwise not join. This status, which could involve a ban on transferring or receiving nuclear explosive devices and acceptance of IAEA safeguards on all peaceful nuclear activities, might apply to countries which had the potential to make nuclear weapons. Such states would reserve the right to proceed to the manufacture and testing of nuclear weapons if they regarded doing so as essential.[4] India and Pakistan have, however, evidently gone well beyond this point. Amending the NPT would in any case be so difficult as to be virtually impossible. Following the tests, William Walker and Michael Quinlan have proposed that India and Pakistan should act as if they were subject to the same obligations as those which the NPT places on its nuclear-weapon state parties.[5] Is there any other method of engaging the two countries?

Both India and Pakistan have a number of civil nuclear reactors which are not subject to IAEA safeguards, and which are neither efficient nor safe.[6] The refusal to accept safeguards is linked to the production by these facilities of fissile material, which could be used for nuclear weapons. An arrangement which allowed for assistance to mitigate the risk of a nuclear accident would, at least in this respect, be of advantage to the wider community, while help in improving the effectiveness of civil nuclear-power programmes would provide a much-needed increase in energy supplies in both India and Pakistan. If arrangements could be found which were consistent with the NPT, and which did not assist nuclear-weapon development, they could induce India and Pakistan to make progress in other related areas.

A second dilemma arises from the conflict between the goal of eliminating nuclear weapons on the subcontinent, and the need to ensure that any existing arsenal is safe and adequately controlled. Here again, the experience of the nuclear-weapon states could be useful. Some methods used to ensure the safety of nuclear warheads are an integral part of their design, and transferring this technology could assist the recipient country to improve the quality of its own designs beyond their safety features. What scope is there for dialogue or exchanges which would not have such unwanted side-effects? Could this dialogue be conducted in ways which did not directly (by contravening Article I) or indirectly (by appearing to accept the *de facto* situation) undermine the NPT?

could dialogue be conducted in ways which did not undermine the NPT?

The relative importance of these considerations is currently unclear; the need for assistance over a technical issue, perhaps involving safety, could for example outweigh the political desirability of being seen to uphold the letter of the non-proliferation regime. A doctrinaire approach from the beginning may thus not be helpful.

Negotiations

After the eighth round of talks between Jaswant Singh and US Deputy Secretary of State Strobe Talbott in February 1999, hopes grew of progress in four of the five key areas identified by the US in November 1998: the CTBT's early signature and ratification; an end to the production of fissile materials for nuclear weapons; export controls; and measures to build confidence and security. The fifth area – strategic restraint – was proving the most intractable. When the talks were halted in April 1999 with the collapse of the BJP-led government, progress was well short of the benchmarks of Resolution 1172. Moreover, as demonstrated by the Kargil crisis, the situation had in some respects deteriorated.

The CTBT

Both India and Pakistan need to be more closely engaged in the international arms-control regime, but without undermining the regime itself in the process. Signing and ratifying the CTBT would reaffirm both countries' commitment to arms-control objectives, which their tests put in doubt. The treaty's moral weight would be seriously weakened if they failed to sign; it could not enter into force without their ratification; and adherence would put pressure on the US to ratify. Domestic politics on the subcontinent could, however, be a serious obstacle. The arguments in India against the CTBT, which from 1996 attracted cross-party support, remain influential. Notwithstanding India's unilateral moratorium, there are lobbies which wish to preserve the country's freedom to test for scientific reasons, for reasons of national sovereignty, or even because doing so is a sign of defiance against outside pressure. The scientific arguments would become stronger if the 1998 tests were not in fact as successful as originally claimed. On the other hand, India's political leadership could argue that, while opposing the CTBT was appropriate before the tests, circumstances had since changed and explosive tests were no longer needed. Moreover, Article IX of the CTBT allows a State Party to withdraw with six months' notice 'if it decides that extraordinary events related to the subject-matter of [the treaty] have jeopardised its supreme interests'.

Pakistan could sign and ratify the CTBT even if India did not do so. If Islamabad were reasonably confident of its capabilities, it would have no need for further tests. There would be rewards in terms of international approval; in addition to the preconditions outlined by Sharif in September 1998 – the removal of sanctions and economic restrictions – Pakistan could also expect increased support for its policy positions, and sympathy for its strategic and economic circumstances. Winning over domestic popular opinion would not, however, be easy, since pressure to be seen to respond to Indian actions would persist.

The CTBT also faces problems beyond the subcontinent. Its unusual requirement that 44 specified countries deposit their instruments of ratification before it can come into force was originally crafted as a means of ensuring that it would not do so without the adherence of all the key states, including India and Pakistan. But this provision also means that the CTBT cannot come into force until all five nuclear-weapon states have ratified it. By late 1999, only the UK and France had done so. As France, Germany and the UK have pointed out, there is clearly a risk that the US Senate's rejection of the CTBT in October 1999 may take the pressure off other still-hesitant countries, including India and Pakistan.[7]

Fissile Materials

The agreement by India and Pakistan to take part in negotiations over a possible fissile-material treaty was reiterated by both countries' foreign ministers at the UN General Assembly in September 1999. This is at least a basis upon which to build. But its significance should not be overestimated, since major obstacles and complications remain, and neither country is showing any zeal. Pakistan is concerned that Indian stockpiles of plutonium reprocessed from spent nuclear-reactor fuel could be used to produce many more warheads than could Pakistan's stocks of enriched uranium obtained from centrifuges. Islamabad has therefore insisted that any fissile-material treaty should encompass current stocks, a condition rejected by New Delhi. One of the key benefits of a fissile-material cut-off treaty would be the arrangements for inspections that it would provide. These have, however, been viewed with suspicion in the subcontinent as intrusions upon national sovereignty, and as a way of 'letting the full-scope safeguards regime gain entry by the back door' by means of intrusive inspections (although it is clear that the verification arrangements for a fissile material cut-off treaty will not amount to this).[8] Moreover, as long as nuclear doctrines in either country remain too under-developed to inform decisions on optimum warhead numbers, each will be reluctant to agree to limits on the production of fissile material. Negotiations, if and when they get under way, will be protracted.

Strategic Restraint

Neither India nor Pakistan has shown any real inclination to slow, still less halt, the development of nuclear-capable missiles and warheads. Both countries, and especially India, have denied that they intend to engage in an arms race, but this simply reflects the view that matching or exceeding the other's arsenal, or acquiring the redundancy that characterised US and Soviet arsenals during the Cold War, is unnecessary. The main requirement in their eyes is independently to develop a credible deterrent. Political exigencies have in any case meant that denials of an arms race have not been borne out in practice. After his country's tests, then Pakistani Foreign Minister Gohar Ayub Khan made a point of observing that Pakistan's six tests and its missile capabilities now gave the country 'the upper edge'.[9] Pakistan's test-firing of the medium-range *Ghauri* I in April 1998 was followed by India's test of the intermediate-range *Agni* II a year later. Within days, Pakistan responded with the first test of the *Ghauri* II and of the shorter-range *Shaheen*, which Islamabad explicitly linked to the *Agni* test, despite the fact that the *Agni* has little relevance to the Indo-Pakistani theatre. Similarly, India shows no sign of slowing its production of *Prithvis*. In April 1999, further tests of the 350km naval version and 250km air-force version were announced, while the 150km-range version has been with army units for several years.[10] These units were initially based at Jullunder, provocatively close to the border with Pakistan, before being relocated to Secunderabad, further to the south.

denials of an arms race have not been borne out in practice

Important aspects of strategic restraint could nonetheless still be agreed. The most significant involve not miniaturising warheads, not deploying missiles within range of key targets and not mating nuclear weapons to their delivery systems. Neither country wants a launch-on-warning strategy which, because of the short flight times involved given the two countries' physical proximity, would entail great costs and enormous risks. There would therefore be advantages in building time-delays into any nuclear escalation. Verification by a third party would not be welcome to either country, particularly where the nuclear arsenals are small, since this could reveal their size and locations. Scope for verification, and hence for enhanced stability, could however increase if tensions eased to the extent that security was less of a preoccupation. Discussion of nuclear doctrines and commitments not to introduce anti-ballistic missiles could also be useful. There is a need too for restraint in the field of conventional forces, which could be encouraged by balanced reductions and the withdrawal of each side's forces from areas of close proximity.

Export Controls

India and Pakistan's control of exports of sensitive materials and technology is essential to prevent other states from developing nuclear weapons, and to maintain global non-proliferation efforts. Both countries are potential suppliers of nuclear- and missile-related items, but neither subscribes to the export-control regimes agreed by the NSG and within the MTCR; rather, they are the targets of these regimes. New Delhi and Islamabad claim that they are punctilious in their maintenance of export controls. India has enacted extensive legislation, and has established procedures to prevent unauthorised nuclear-related exports. There does not appear to be any evidence that such exports have taken place. The fact that industries in this field are state-controlled clearly makes the task easier. But the relevant legislation is formulated in broad terms; bringing it more into line with international standards would be a significant gesture of solidarity with global efforts.

Pakistan's nuclear industry is also state-controlled, and here too no evidence has emerged of exports of sensitive material or technology. In May 1999, Sharif reiterated that, as a 'consistent policy', Pakistan would not transfer nuclear technology or material to any other country or entity.[11] The Pakistani leadership took pains to dismiss boasts of a so-called 'Islamic Bomb', which had suggested that Pakistan might share its capabilities with other Islamic countries. But there is no significant legislation in this area, and international concerns were raised by a visit to the Kahuta uranium-enrichment plant by Saudi Defence Minister Prince Sultan bin Abdul Aziz al-Saud in May 1999. It is possible that Pakistan could supply North Korea with nuclear-weapon technology received from China, in exchange for missile technology in lieu of payment in hard currency. Such concerns could be baseless, but legislation would nonetheless help to put them to rest.

Confidence-Building

Since independence, India and Pakistan have periodically sought to improve relations, but progress has been disappointing. In the early 1990s, as tensions grew in the Kashmir Valley following the end of the Afghan war, proposals concentrated on military-to-military agreements. Emphasis then shifted to trade, cultural links and people-to-people contacts. Negotiations stalled in 1994, but were renewed in early 1997, when talks were held between Indian Foreign Secretary Salman Haidar and his Pakistani counterpart, Shamsad Ahmad. In June 1997, agreement was reached on establishing working groups to tackle eight issues: peace and security, including confidence-building measures; Jammu and Kashmir; the Siachen Glacier; the Wullar Barrage/Tulbul Navigation Project, where there is dispute over the use of water resources; the Sir Creek boundary dispute; terrorism and drug-trafficking; economic and commercial cooperation; and the promotion of friendly exchanges. The following month, the two countries released several hundred fishermen detained for violation of territorial waters, some of whom had been held for four years, and travel and trade restrictions were eased. But progress faltered as tensions at the Line of Control rose again during the summer, and the formation of the working groups hit a procedural impasse shortly before the fall of Inder Kumar Gujral's United Front government in November.

The need to improve regional stability frequently clashes with domestic political pressure to demonstrate that national interests are being protected. Immediately after the Lahore meeting in February 1999, and the two sides' commitment to 'intensify their efforts to resolve all issues', both India and Pakistan made plain to their respective publics that their fundamental positions had not changed. At a meeting with Pakistani President Rafiq Tarar the day after the Lahore agreement, visiting Chinese Defence Minister Chi Haotian expressed support for Islamabad's position on Kashmir, inflaming Indian opinion at least as much as it reassured constituents in Pakistan.[12] The *Agni* test in April 1999, which took place at a time when the BJP-led government was in an exceptionally precarious position, showed that limitations to any 'Lahore spirit' existed on both sides. Although not breaching the undertaking to give advance warning of such tests, India notified Pakistan only two days beforehand, at the same time as it informed other countries – and only after Pakistan's High Commissioner in New Delhi had made official enquiries about press reports of warnings to shipping and air-traffic-control authorities in India. At the time of the tests in 1998, existing confidence- and security-building measures were neglected. Hotlines between the two prime ministers were not used, and it was only some days after the alarm was raised in Pakistan about a possible Indian–Israeli attack on the country's Kahuta facility that attention was drawn to a 1988 agreement between New Delhi and Islamabad not to attack each other's nuclear installations.

Kashmir is at the heart of the differences between India and Pakistan. Since the issue poses risks to wider stability, it is also of concern to other countries. It is commonly held internationally that human-rights abuse by Indian security forces and outside help to militants in Kashmir should both cease, and that the views of the area's people should be more fully taken into account. However, direct third-party involvement would require the consent not just of Pakistan, but also of India, which is improbable. This increases the importance of dialogue between New Delhi and Islamabad, and of restraint from both sides. India maintains that progress over issues other than Kashmir would improve the atmosphere and make Kashmir itself a less intractable problem. Pakistan, on the other hand, regards such an approach as consolidating the status quo; for Islamabad, Kashmir is the 'core issue'. This dilemma needs to be resolved.

The apparent failure fundamentally to improve relations does not mean that confidence- and security-building measures are without value (see Appendix, page 75). Agreement on such measures does not in itself guarantee that they will be adhered to. But they can, and frequently do, exert moral pressure, and can be useful indicators of incipient problems during times of tension. Despite setbacks and a period of scepticism in the mid-1990s, opinion was shifting in favour of dialogue before the 1998 tests. The fact that Vajpayee and Sharif spoke by telephone during the Kargil crisis suggested a new awareness of the value of confidence-building measures.[13] Several other measures received new attention, including India's possible purchase of power generated in Pakistan. If this happened, it could mark a genuine step forward since it would mean India's acceptance of a degree of dependence on its neighbour for an important resource. In turn, Pakistan would need to accept that progress on Kashmir might take second place to developing confidence and a degree of interdependence.[14] However, dialogue on this issue was set back badly by the Kargil crisis.

Outside Actors
The United States
Progress in fulfilling the benchmarks of Resolution 1172 will depend both on the policies of India and Pakistan, and on the extent to

which outside influence can be brought to bear. Of all outside governments, the US has been the most closely engaged with the subcontinent since the tests. Although appropriate and practicable given the breadth of its interests and influence, US involvement is a source of controversy in both countries, irrespective of the tact and sensitivity of individual negotiators. Anti-American sentiment is seldom far from the surface, and can be used as a basis for nationalist or populist appeals for resistance. Clinton's agreement with Sharif during the Kargil conflict was even criticised in India as an 'inter-nationalisation' of what New Delhi insists is a bilateral matter.[15]

US involvement is a source of controversy

India has long been dismayed by what it regards as the United States' pro-Pakistan leanings, and its failure to recognise India's perceived proper status. This grievance is especially pointed given Washington's apparent deference towards Beijing. Pakistan meanwhile feels that it has been unfairly treated by the US after its cooperation during the war in Afghanistan, and discriminated against by legislation preventing it from acquiring the wherewithal to defend itself against its neighbour. For example, Pakistan points to US agreements with India in 1982 and 1984 – a Memorandum of Understanding on Sensitive Technologies, Commodities and Information and the Reagan–Gandhi Science and Technology Initiative. Both were reached while Islamabad was subject to sanctions. On the other hand, India argues that the US turned a blind eye to Pakistan's acquisition of a nuclear-weapon capability until Washington's strategic interests had changed, and the administration had no option but to withhold certification that such a capability did not exist.

Considerations such as these help to explain the line taken by Indian officials towards discussions with the US. With the exception of its call for restraint in the development and deployment of nuclear weapons, the five priority areas identified by the US in 1998 chimed with actions or policies specified by India, either at the time of its tests or shortly afterwards. With a little blurring of the distinction between declarations of intent and concrete action, the Indian authorities could thus claim that they were, up to a point, heeding international demands, and should be rewarded accordingly. (One especially disingenuous argument holds that the West should in fact be grateful to India for the contribution that its tests have made to non-proliferation efforts, because India and Pakistan might as a result sign up to the CTBT.) India was engaged in dialogue with the US because Washington was acting on behalf of a wider international constituency, which it would have been churlish to ignore. This approach has its uses in managing domestic Indian opinion, but it could also make progress well-nigh impossible by creating an antagonistic political climate.

Pakistan's approach has been different. Islamabad cannot pretend to match Indian aspirations for international status, and so has presented itself as the injured party. In a speech to the UN General Assembly in September 1999, Foreign Minister Aziz gave a high priority to the lifting of economic sanctions, and to persuading the international community to press India over its nuclear plans. Aziz also pointed out that progress over Kashmir, as advocated by the international community, was impossible unless his country's underlying security concerns were addressed.[16]

China

India's nuclear tests raised fundamental questions about the state of relations with China, and how they would develop. Had the ten-year-old policy of *rapprochement* fallen victim to India's coalition politics, leaving long-term strategic planning in a vacuum? What basis was there for India's concern about China? To what extent could relations be improved, and how? India's grievances were many, and simply managing differences without any visible progress or real engagement seemed insufficient. New Delhi's concerns about China's nuclear cooperation with Pakistan were understandable, and frustration over perceived Chinese arrogance was allowed to boil over publicly before and after the tests. However, the argument that China posed a real threat was not convincing. Chinese weaponry was not directed at India, and none of the disagreements between the two countries was causing significant problems. Status, rather than substance, seemed to be at stake.

India may, however, see deeper reasons for concern. China's economic, diplomatic and military weight, and its strategically important geographical position, have all contributed to its international status – a status out of India's reach for many years, the country's population growth and democratic system notwith-standing. The report issued by a US House of Representatives committee chaired by Republican Christopher Cox in March 1999, alleging Chinese nuclear espionage in the US, will not have eased Indian worries about its neighbour's growing military capabilities. This, together with China's strong opposition to US proposals for national missile defence in Asia, has been used by India as retrospective justification for its tests, and for its delay in signing the CTBT.

India's public commitment to developing a strategic nuclear deterrent against China suggests that the relationship is unlikely to remain static. Will India regard the *Agni* III, which could reach major Chinese population centres, as sufficient 'minimum deterrence'? Or will it opt for a submarine-based deterrent, as advocated in a draft report released by the National Security Advisory Board (NSAB) in August 1999? How would India respond to a Chinese threat to use a tactical nuclear weapon in the Himalayas? If India's arsenal were developed so as to provide a China-related deterrent, Pakistan would be likely to try to keep pace. If China did the same, India could be forced into still-further enhancement of its nuclear capability. A dangerous and expensive spiral could take shape.

Given these grim possibilities, India's attempts to patch up its differences with China in 1999 were prudent, and Beijing has proved more receptive to these overtures than its stance in 1998 suggested. The common ground on which the two countries might build is nonetheless limited. Shared interests are relatively few, and have tended to be submerged by nationalism on both sides. Despite ten-fold growth since 1992, bilateral trade, which stood at $2bn in 1998, remains tiny in Chinese terms, although this could change as India's economy develops. Both Beijing and New Delhi have declared an interest in 'multipolarity' in opposition to US and Western dominance, but in China this is often expressed in terms of 'saving' others from US 'hegemony'. This sits uneasily with attempts by New Delhi and Washington to improve their relations, which could lead Beijing to imagine a US strategy of containment via India. China's links with Pakistan, especially nuclear and missile cooperation, will remain the touchstone for India. Beijing may not wish to end its long-standing friendship with Islamabad, but it could adopt a more balanced approach to both India and Pakistan. 'Normal' relations between two such large neighbours as India and China are probably too much to hope for, particularly while border disputes persist, but they should be able to manage their differences more prudently.

Limited progress in some areas of arms control has been made in the wake of the tests, despite political turbulence in India and Pakistan and the wider problems over the CTBT. India's relations with the international community have stabilised sufficiently to allow constructive dialogue to take place. But India and China need to break down their mutual distrust, while neither India nor Pakistan will contemplate limiting their development and production of nuclear weapons before major obstacles are overcome.

chapter 4

Nuclear Capabilities, Nuclear Doctrines

Decision-making in a nuclear environment demands the utmost coherence, rationality and efficiency. As Michael Quinlan put it in 1997, the coming of nuclear weapons 'carries the potential of warfare past a boundary at which many previous conceptions and categories of appraisal – both military and political – ceased to apply, or even to have meaning'.[1] However, neither India nor Pakistan has fully explained how nuclear weapons would enhance their security, and early official statements on nuclear strategy were scanty. The confusion on this subject was acknowledged by Jaswant Singh in 1998, when he referred in his book *Defending India* to the questionable deterrent value of nuclear weapons that were 'not really useable'.[2] It was also reflected in the subsequent Indian admission that nuclear doctrines had still to be developed. In dismissing Cold War practices as irrelevant, Indian and Pakistani leaders and commentators appeared to blur the distinction between deterrence and defence, contending that simply possessing a nuclear capability would be sufficient in itself, without any apparent need for weapon systems that might actually be used.

A year after the tests, doubts had emerged in India as to the credibility of a deterrence which rested on little more than basic capabilities and a claim to the status of a nuclear-weapon power. The Kargil conflict of 1999 focused attention on the related question of what to do if deterrence failed.[3] Pressure grew to enhance the country's nuclear and conventional forces in order to provide a visibly effective means of surviving a nuclear first strike, and to ensure a punitive response. Nonetheless, by the time the BJP returned to power in October 1999 many questions remained. What were the threats? How would the decision-making process be assured in the event of a pre-emptive strike? Would there be delegation to individuals other than the prime minister? How would decisions be communicated? How would communication links be protected? What delivery vehicles and how many warheads would be needed? How would they be protected? What measures would be taken to ensure against unauthorised or accidental use, for instance in the event of a breakdown in communications with local commanders? What would all this cost, and was it affordable?[4]

Capabilities

According to India's DAE and Defence Research and Development Organisation (DRDO), the country's first test, on 11 May, involved the simultaneous detonation of a fission device with a yield of about 12 kilotons; a thermonuclear device of about 43kt; and a sub-kiloton device. On 13 May, two more devices were simultaneously detonated, with a yield of 0.2–0.6kt.[5] According to Defence Minister Fernandes, no further tests were required; Abdul Kalam, the head of India's missile-development programme, told a press conference on 17 May that 'weaponisation' was 'complete'. The fissile material used in the tests was, according to the DEA and DRDO, completely indigenous. Other authoritative Indian sources claimed that the 43kt device was 'third generation' – a new design of fission bomb, small in size and weight, but high in yield. R. Chidambaram, the chairman of India's AEC, stated that a fission explosion had been used to trigger a fusion one; a 'boosted fission' weapon was available, but had not been tested, apparently out of concern for the effects on nearby population centres. Finally, P. K. Iyengar, a former AEC chairman, claimed in October 1998 that three categories of device were involved: low-yield tactical; full-size fission; and thermo-nuclear.[6]

Initial foreign estimates based on seismic evidence suggested that actual yields amounted to about ten kilotons for the first three combined tests, while nothing was registered for the second set of sub-kiloton tests. This cast doubt on Indian claims that the total yield was more than 55kt, and that a thermonuclear device, which experts believed would have shown a higher yield, had been successfully tested. Estimates were later revised upwards to between 25kt and 30kt. Although lower than the Indian claim, these later figures were not sufficiently low to challenge directly the assertion that a thermonuclear explosion had taken place.[7] However, other later estimates did suggest yields sufficiently low to cast further doubt on India's ability to design and successfully detonate a hydrogen bomb.[8]

Similar uncertainties surround the actual number of warheads available to India, and the size of its stocks of fissile material. Analysis in 1996 had estimated that India's stockpile of separated weapon-grade plutonium in the preceding year was 330 kilograms, plus or minus 30% – enough for at least 65, and possibly as many as 90, weapons.[9] India may be able to produce 20kg of separated plutonium a year, which could give it more than 100 warheads by 2005. In 1998, the US Natural Resources Defense Council (NRDC) suggested that proven designs existed for a two-stage thermonuclear weapon, a standard fission weapon of between ten and 15kt, and a smaller (2–3kt) weapon. The NRDC also estimated that India had enough material for up to 50 warheads.[10] In 1999, the Congressional Research Service put the number at 75 or more. By reprocessing fuel from its nuclear reactors, India could theoretically have obtained enough plutonium for between 390 and 470 warheads.[11] India can also produce tritium, which could be used for hydrogen bombs. But estimates are no more than that: little is known about India's nuclear programme, particularly its unsafeguarded reactors.

Of the delivery vehicles being developed, the most significant are the medium-range *Prithvi* and intermediate-range *Agni* missiles, of which only the *Prithvi* has been extensively tested. It is unclear whether India could deploy a two-stage nuclear weapon or boosted-fission device on a ballistic missile. Until the country's missiles and their associated warheads have been fully developed, aircraft will be the primary delivery system. Sea-launched missiles, carried by surface ships such as the *Delhi*-class destroyer or by nuclear submarines, would be more valuable in relation to China than Pakistan. Nuclear artillery may not be an attractive option because of the difficulties of miniaturising warheads, the relatively large amount of fissile material involved, and the cost.

Given that it has probably benefited from tests conducted by other countries, Pakistan's nuclear and missile capabilities may be relatively proven and reliable. On 31 May, the head of the country's nuclear programme, Abdul Qadeer Khan, claimed that all six of his country's tests had involved boosted fission devices using uranium 235. Cumulative yields were 50kt, comprising one detonation of 25kt, two of 12kt and three with sub-kiloton yields.[12] Here again, however, seismic evidence suggested lower yields, with the first set of tests amounting to between six and 16kt, and the second 4–6kt. Stocks of fissile material, believed to be highly enriched uranium produced at the centrifuge plant at Kahuta, may amount to between 400kg and 600kg, which could be sufficient for 20–30 weapons.[13] There are, however, other estimates: between ten and 15 weapons, according to the Congressional Research Service; the NRDC suggests that Pakistan has sufficient material to arm a dozen weapons, and designs for weapons of between 30kt and 35kt.[14] In October 1998, analyst Ian Steer suggested that Pakistan was able to produce more than 100 bombs.[15] Pakistan, like India, is developing nuclear-capable missiles, the most significant of which are the *Ghauri* and the M-11.

Doctrines

Official Indian statements about doctrine have been sketchy, and it is likely that little thought was given to the issue before the tests took place.[16] The main elements announced by Vajpayee in May 1998 were:

- India would not use nuclear weapons for aggression, or to threaten any other country;
- nuclear weapons were for self-defence, and aimed to ensure that India was not subject to nuclear threats or coercion;
- India would not engage in an arms race;
- India would observe a voluntary moratorium on underground test explosions;
- resources were available to ensure a credible deterrent; and
- India was ready to discuss a no-first-use agreement with Pakistan.[17]

In July, Fernandes was quoted as saying that the country's nuclear weapons were for strategic deterrence, not tactical use.[18] The following month, in a statement to the lower house of parliament, Vajpayee declared that India 'will have a policy of a minimum deterrent'; that the country would not be the first to use nuclear weapons, and would not use them against a non-nuclear-weapon state; and that command-and-control lay with the country's political leadership, and would always remain in civilian hands. Jaswant Singh also stressed that the tests were 'not directed against any country'. In October, India put forward a proposal in the UN General Assembly for concerted action to reduce the risks of unintentional or accidental use of nuclear weapons, and drew attention to the dangers of 'hair-trigger alerts' and 'launch-on-warning' strategies.

The careful language of such pre-prepared statements conflicted with other, less circumspect pronouncements. Although doing little more than highlighting the obvious fact that the countries of most concern to India were China and Pakistan, the singling out of China as posing the main threat, together with Home Minister L. K. Advani's pledge on 12 May to 'deal firmly and strongly with Pakistan's designs and its activities in Kashmir', did not sit well with the claim that the tests were not directed at any countries in particular, or with the assertion that the weapons were not meant to be threatening. The presence of Farooq Abdullah, Chief Minister of Jammu and Kashmir, during Vajpayee's visit to the test site at Pokhran on 20 May could scarcely have sent a clearer signal to Islamabad.

Reflecting the need to develop a doctrine, in November 1998 Vajpayee established a three-tier structure to undertake a strategic defence review, and to decide on long-term policy options. This structure comprised a 27-strong National Security Council, chaired by the prime minister; a Strategic Policy Group involving senior officials and the heads of the three armed services; and the NSAB, under K. Subrahmanyam's chairmanship.[19] In August 1999, during the campaign for the forthcoming general elections, the caretaker government released a six-page draft NSAB document outlining 'the broad principles for the development and deployment of India's nuclear forces'. The document set out a justification of India's nuclear tests, and argued that the country should pursue a doctrine of credible minimum deterrence within a policy of 'retaliation only'. The characteristics of nuclear forces would be decided in the light of the strategic environment, technological imperatives and national security needs, but would be based on a triad of aircraft, mobile land-based missiles and sea-based assets, plus command, control and intelligence systems. The report also stated that it should be possible 'to shift from peacetime deployment to fully employable forces in the shortest possible time'. The authority to release nuclear weapons would rest with the prime minister 'or designated successors'. Nuclear forces would need to survive a surprise attack, a first strike and 'repetitive attrition attempts', while retaining 'adequate retaliatory capabilities'. Finally, effective conventional military capabilities should also be maintained, and space-based assets established for early-warning, communications and damage assessment.[20]

India's elaboration of its nuclear policy in the year following the tests appeared to be designed to reassure international opinion about the country's intentions. It conveyed three messages. First, the pre-test situation of 'opaque' deterrence had not really changed, and the West was over-reacting. Second, fears of an arms race were unjustified, and the arrangements made during the Cold War were not relevant to South Asia. The West did not understand the situation on the subcontinent, which was as capable of managing its affairs as had been the protagonists of the Cold War. India should be credited with as much good sense as any other country, and needed no lessons in how to act. The country's rejection of launch-on-warning strategies showed that it fully recognised the risks inherent in a hair-trigger response. At bottom, it was implied, Western criticism was racist.[21] India was a major power, and should be treated as such. Third, India did not intend to impoverish itself by emulating the extensive and costly capabilities possessed by the US and the Soviet Union during the Cold War. An effective deterrent could be obtained without significant cost to development efforts. There was thus no reason for foreign investors to be discouraged from pursuing commercial opportunities in India. The budget of March 1999, in contrast to the previous year's, reinforced this message by giving a new impetus to economic liberalisation. Having proved its nationalist credentials, the BJP could afford to be less defensive about liberalisation, which would attract Western investors and mute Western criticism.

Nonetheless, significant questions remained after the BJP's return to power in October 1999. The NSAB report suggested a much larger and more operationally ready deterrent force than official statements after the tests had implied, and there was a large shortfall between the NSAB's recommendations and the country's actual capabilities. The document said little about the nature of command-and-control arrangements, or about how nuclear weapons would be made to survive attack. It also shed no light on arrangements for authorising the use of nuclear weapons beyond the opaque reference to the prime minister or 'designated successors'. Crucially, it gave no estimates of what deterrence would cost.

In the wake of the tests, Pakistan's statements concentrated on criticising India, rather than elaborating a doctrine. In May 1998, Sharif claimed that Pakistan had been 'obliged to exercise the nuclear option due to the weaponisation of India's nuclear programme. This had led to the collapse of the "existential deterrence" and had radically altered the strategic balance in our region'. The decision was taken 'in the interest of national self defence. These weapons are to deter aggression, whether nuclear or conventional'; Pakistan had 'instituted command and control structures'.[22] Sharif's linkage of Pakistan's nuclear weapons with possible aggression by conventional forces plainly allowed for their first-use, without limiting them to deterring Indian nuclear threats. This position was subsequently reiterated in official statements.[23] In July, Ambassador Munir Akram, Pakistan's representative at the Conference on Disarmament in Geneva, stated that Islamabad had 'concluded that a situation of mutual deterrence now exists between India and Pakistan. Pakistan will seek to maintain this situation of deterrence in future. The level at which this is maintained will be determined in accordance with any escalatory steps taken by India'. Pakistan had an interest in maintaining nuclear deterrence 'at the lowest possible level', while ensuring against 'strategic vulnerability in certain areas – such as fissile materials and ballistic missiles'. Akram endorsed the declared objective of the UN Security Council's Permanent Members and the G-8 to convince India not to deploy weaponised delivery systems. This in fact applied to both countries, but Akram gave no undertaking that Pakistan would not deploy such systems. He also suggested that Pakistan's economic difficulties, embargoes 'by some major powers' and India's arms acquisitions had contributed to an 'asymmetry in conventional weapons capabilities'.[24] Responding to the publication of the NSAB report, Pakistan's Foreign Minister Aziz stated on 18 August that his country's doctrine would be based on the proposed regime of strategic nuclear restraint discussed with India in 1998.[25]

Minimum Deterrence

Statements by both India and Pakistan suggested that each was aiming for a policy of minimum deterrence. However, in practice the concept has been subject to widely differing interpretations. Minimum deterrence requires not only the ability to launch nuclear weapons, but also a judgement about the number and nature of weapons necessary to deter a potential adversary. This judgement may alter with changing perceptions of the potential threat, and opinions are thus bound to differ. Several Indian and Western commentators have argued that it can be sufficient for the purposes of deterrence for a potential aggressor to recognise the merest possibility that a nuclear weapon will be successfully launched, evade defences, strike its target, detonate and cause a high and unacceptable level of destruction.[26] There is therefore no need for sophisticated command-and-control arrangements, or for extensive efforts to ensure the survivability of all delivery vehicles. Warheads are relatively easy to protect, and sufficient numbers of delivery vehicles would be available to make it reasonably likely that some at least would get through an adversary's defences.

minimum deterrence has been subject to widely differing interpretations

Although the Indian government has revealed no objectives for the size of the country's nuclear arsenal, the official position appears broadly consistent with this argument, despite the many questions that it begs. IDSA director Jasjit Singh defines minimum deterrence as 'the lowest level of weapons that can cause death and destruction which, if imposed on the adversary, would deter it'.[27] (This is similar to Western definitions. Lawrence Freedman, for example, defines minimum deterrence as 'the possession of sufficient nuclear weapons to inflict grievous harm on the enemy in retaliation, but no more'.)[28] Singh further suggests that deterrence can effectively function at levels below the minimum; his theory of 'recessed deterrence' involves the possession of credible capabilities, including delivery systems and unassembled warheads, but falls short of actual weaponisation (by which Singh appears to mean making nuclear weapons operational). The option to weaponise would be kept open; exercising it would depend upon the level of threat. Singh argues that two to three dozen warheads, acquired over ten or 15 years, would suffice for the purposes of recessed deterrence.[29]

According to Singh, achieving recessed deterrence would require that all the necessary steps for weaponisation should have been taken; but the extent of readiness should normally be kept classified. This would involve a high degree of ambiguity. One of the positive aspects of this idea, Singh argues, is that 'recessed' or non-weaponised deterrence could, depending upon the political environment, be maintained almost indefinitely, and could ultimately be reversed if progress were made in global nuclear disarmament. But there are also problems with this concept. For recessed deterrence to be credible, India would need to be able to shift to overt deterrence in step with any escalation of political tension or threat which, in South Asia, could be very swift. To do this would require considerable development of the capabilities that India currently has, both in terms of hardware and command-and-control systems.

Jasjit Singh's predecessor at IDSA, K. Subrahmanyam, has argued that deterrence would be best assured by targeting the adversary's population centres, rather than its nuclear facilities, and nuclear war-fighting would not be an objective. Only a simple deployment pattern would be needed, with uncomplicated targeting and relatively primitive command, control and intelligence arrangements. The force could consist of 60 125kt warheads, to be delivered by aircraft or by *Prithvi* and *Agni* missiles. A minimal capability against China would serve purely to prevent nuclear blackmail.[30] Others have argued for more extensive capabilities. Brahma Chellaney suggests that a deterrent against Pakistan 'was never the central mission of India's nuclear strategy', and argues that India 'can effectively deter Beijing … with less than 100 warheads'.[31] Brigadier Vijai Nair favours a triad of delivery systems, comprising aircraft and ground- and submarine-launched missiles, and argues for 132 warheads of differing yields.[32] Bharat Karnad goes further, suggesting that India should aim for nothing less than what he describes as notional parity with the UK, France and China: between

350 and 400 weapons or warheads.[33] While an increasingly vocal lobby in both India and Pakistan has argued against the possession of nuclear weapons, and criticised the decisions to test, the extent of its influence is unclear.[34]

Evolving Doctrines and Capabilities

It need not be assumed that India's more hawkish commentators greatly influenced the decision to test, or that their ideas will prevail in future, since several non-military motives lay behind the country's bid for nuclear status. But the declaration of this status has given new impetus to thinking about doctrine on the subcontinent. Vijai Nair among others has pointed to 'a need to enhance the attributes of security management in keeping with the changes brought about by India's nuclear tests'.[35] The debate has still to be concluded, and many options remain open. India's doctrine could evolve to the point where full weaponisation and the deployment of large numbers of weapons and delivery vehicles took place. Alternatively, capabilities and dispositions could remain unclear. Parliamentarians, largely uninvolved hitherto, will want their say. The Indian military, although not party to the decision to test, will nonetheless regard it as its duty to address the strategic, tactical and operational implications of possessing nuclear capabilities. Whereas in India, proponents of testing acted outside of government in an attempt to influence it, in Pakistan the military was closely involved in issues of nuclear strategy. The nature of the public debate in each country reflects this key difference, and few issues of doctrine have been publicly aired in Pakistan.

the declaration of nuclear status has given new impetus to thinking about doctrine on the subcontinent

If there is any tendency on the part of political leaders to believe, or hope, that the mere possession of a nuclear capability will suffice as a deterrent, others will press for greater clarity, and will advance proposals to provide it. This pressure will be felt most immediately as more missiles become available for deployment. Decisions will be called for on their allocation, positioning, mobility and storage. Military commanders will want to draw up contingency plans and proceed with training, both to ensure efficiency in managing their responsibilities and to maximise safety. Any technical difficulties will provoke calls for more resources to overcome them. Similarly, there will be pressure for aircraft earmarked for nuclear-weapon delivery to be fitted out, positioned and protected. Commanders will also want contingency plans covering authorisation arrangements, operational safety and targeting. Meanwhile, it is unlikely that either India or Pakistan has a clear idea of the other's capabilities. New tensions would arise if one assessed that it had underestimated the other.

Retaliation and No-First-Use

India's declaration of a no-first-use policy in July 1998 is of limited significance. It has not been underpinned by any legal obligation and, if circumstances warranted, could simply be ignored. Since India has evidently been unimpressed by China's no-first-use declaration, it has little basis to expect a warmer response from others. Given Pakistan's known concern about India's conventional military superiority, New Delhi's proposal that Islamabad should join it in a formal commitment to no-first-use looks much like a political ploy.

The indications are that India will concentrate on developing and maintaining a credible policy of 'retaliation after ride-out' – that is, after absorbing a first strike. If this is the case, the proposition that nuclear weapons 'are not really usable' will be hard to sustain given that deterrence requires the possibility, even if remote, that these weapons could actually be used. As Bruce G. Blair has pointed out, the burden of retaliation falls on complex strategic organisations whose basic coherence is threatened by opposing nuclear forces.[36] How does India convince others that it would still be able to retaliate after absorbing a first strike? Pakistan's position is different. Islamabad has not ruled out nuclear first-use as a means of deterring attack by Indian conventional forces, or in the face of a nuclear threat. During the Kargil conflict, Sharif claimed that Pakistan was 'fully equipped' to meet any nuclear threat from India, and Aziz stated that 'we will not hesitate to use any weapon in our arsenal to defend our territorial integrity'. Both declarations were interpreted as veiled nuclear threats.[37] Pakistan's lack of strategic depth and the strength of India's conventional forces, especially aircraft, mean that Pakistani leaders might consider that early nuclear use would prevent the likely erosion by an Indian conventional attack of their strike and command-and-control capabilities. Such a posture would of course be highly dangerous, particularly given the proximity of the two countries. A supposed need for rapid reaction, a misjudgement or a misunderstanding would have disastrous consequences. In the heat of a political crisis, there might be only a narrow margin between a response to a perceived violation of a frontier and a pre-emptive strike to forestall it.

Eric Arnett has suggested that there are risks of a dangerous mismatch between each country's perception of what the other would do during a crisis.[38] Since Pakistan is at a military disadvantage, in order to maintain deterrence it has an interest in appearing to be ready to use nuclear weapons at an early stage if it felt itself to be vitally threatened. But Indian leaders might believe that Pakistan would hold back from early use for fear of massive Indian nuclear retaliation, and out of concern not to break the 'nuclear taboo'. India might therefore choose to deal with Pakistani support for militancy within Kashmir, for instance, by using conventional weapons in a counter-force mode outside the area. This in turn could lead to a nuclear response from Pakistan. The settlement of the Kargil confrontation should not be taken as proof that this risk is exaggerated.

India has denied any role for battlefield nuclear weapons, concentrating instead on a counter-value function directed at population centres. Jasjit Singh argues that, if 'a physical neighbour' were to initiate a nuclear exchange, it should expect grave consequences; there is no such thing as a tactical nuclear weapon in this context.[39] But would a threat of nuclear retaliation against a major population centre be a credible deterrent against the use of a low-yield device on a battlefield?

Command-and-Control

In the absence of any details or apparent preparation, Indian and Pakistani claims that they already possess command-and-control systems are questionable. Several Indian commentators, notably General K. Sundarji and Vijai Nair, have drawn attention to alleged deficiencies in current structures. Kapil Kak, Senior Fellow at IDSA, has suggested that the essential elements should comprise:

- a 'highly survivable national command' during a crisis or conflict;
- robust, fail-safe and survivable communications between the command and strategic nuclear forces;
- strategic intelligence, surveillance, reconnaissance, warning and damage assessment, allowing 'situational evaluation before, during and after an adversary's first strike'; and
- the wide dispersion of strategic nuclear forces, increasing the possibility that some units will survive an adversary's 'disarming attack'.[40]

Kak has suggested that examining the structures of the 'traditional' nuclear powers could help India to evolve its own doctrine, whilst avoiding heavy expenditure, which it cannot afford. The delay between absorbing a first strike and retaliation should be no greater than 24 hours; waiting any longer could allow international pressure to erode the foundations of India's deterrence.

Pakistani literature is relatively silent on command-and-control issues, although the subject has been under active debate, suggesting that it still needs refining. In April 1999, Musharraf, Pakistan's Chief of Army Staff, announced that the Joint Staff Headquarters was to have a command-and-control arrangement and secretariat, with wide powers over nuclear issues such as the CTBT and missile-related technology. A strategic-force command would also be established.[41] Other reports suggested that the Defence Cabinet Committee would be used, thereby strengthening civilian control. The coup in October 1999 has raised additional questions concerning accountability and nuclear responsibilities, not least since the positions of Chief of Army Staff, Chief of Joint Staff Headquarters and Chief Executive of the country are all held by Musharraf alone.

Technical Issues, Safety and Affordability
For reasons of national prestige and in order to enhance deterrence, governments seek to convey the impression that they have mastered the scientific and technical problems surrounding nuclear weapons. However, the technical capabilities needed to make nuclear devices safe are much greater than those required to cause a nuclear

explosion. Basic nuclear weapons, like those of the early years of the Cold War, may not incorporate the safety features or other devices designed to prevent premature or accidental explosion. Permissive Action Links (PALs) in warheads, coding and authentication systems to prevent unauthorised use and measures to disarm after an initial order has been given require still more advanced technical knowledge.

The risks of accidental or unauthorised detonation are real. In a crisis in which communications have broken down, a squadron commander could come under pressure to safeguard his aircraft and personnel by ordering them airborne, raising the risk of accident or attack. Either event could cause a nuclear detonation if the aircraft were carrying unsophisticated nuclear weapons. This is not, as Paul Bracken notes, an issue of the 'mad-commander' type; during the Korean War of 1950–53, for example, Bracken recounts precisely this dilemma facing a US squadron commander, each of whose F-100 aircraft was carrying a one-megaton bomb which 'had too high a risk of going off if it were dropped or if there were an accident'.[42] Bracken's anecdote illustrates the genuine and difficult choices that could face rational commanders in the field.

The effects of an accidental detonation would be felt well beyond its immediate area, and could lead to a nuclear exchange. National commanders need to know whether a nuclear detonation on or near their territory was accidental, or was the result of an adversary's strike, if they are to prevent premature retaliation. These questions need to be addressed, and the appropriate mechanisms put in place, well before nuclear weapons are deployed. If the available technical expertise is insufficient to do this, strategy and dispositions need to be framed accordingly. While the skill, inventiveness and resourcefulness of both India and Pakistan are not in question, there are doubts as to the extent to which safety-related problems have been resolved. Both countries appear to have developed their nuclear capabilities in a rush, and safety may not have been a high priority. The signs of technical limitations – deficient nuclear-power plants, problems in the development of the *Arjun* tank and Light Combat Aircraft in India, and the discrepancies between the claimed yields of the nuclear tests and the seismic evidence – can only heighten safety concerns.

Similar questions surround the affordability of equipment, safety measures and command-and-control systems. Both India and Pakistan have acquired modern military hardware, including dual-capable aircraft, from foreign suppliers. Pakistan's nuclear and missile programmes have allegedly received Chinese and North Korean help, while India's missile development, although relying apparently on its own resources, has probably drawn on the skills developed in its civil satellite work. If China honours the undertakings given to the US in May 1996 not to provide assistance to countries with unsafeguarded nuclear facilities, and ceases its reported help to Pakistan, technical development may become significantly more challenging.[43] Difficulties would also increase if the international controls on the transfer of missile technology were toughened in the light of the increased tensions in the region. Refining missile programmes is more difficult and expensive than acquiring aircraft, while the complexity and cost involved in developing nuclear submarines and associated missiles are so high as to make Indian claims to such a capability in the near future little more than bravado. Karnad, for example, claims that an Indian-designed and -manufactured submarine, able to fire an indigenous ballistic missile, should be in service by 2010.[44]

To the costs of developing nuclear capabilities must be added those of maintaining them. US spending, estimated to have been more than $5 trillion, conveys an idea of the massive expense which can be involved.[45] The UK's *Trident* programme, which enjoyed considerable US assistance, cost some £12.5bn, while in the 1997–98 financial year, the UK spent £410m on its (considerably reduced) nuclear-warhead programme.[46] Spending on sophisticated equipment and the search for solutions to technical problems could be open-ended, and much of it ultimately fruitless. If decisions on hardware procurement were based upon assumptions that safety problems would be solved before the hardware was due to enter service, but, in the event, hardware was produced without these problems being resolved, the result could be both expensive and highly dangerous.

There are many uncertainties and dangers surrounding concepts of nuclear deterrence in the subcontinent; policy will take some time to develop, and will be subject to change. Minimum deterrence in South Asia is ill-defined, and offers little guidance to those responsible for developing and maintaining its instruments. Pressures are building, especially in India, for greater clarity and for enhancements to the nuclear arsenal. Although the absence of well-defined doctrines increases the risk of misunderstanding and misjudgement, there are strong political, economic and military arguments against clarifying deterrence policies and actual capabilities. A balance needs to be struck between these competing factors. Areas of particular concern include technical safety arrangements built into the design of the devices; adequate means of protecting them from detonation in the event of attack; and fail-safe command-and-control arrangements.

conclusion

What Should Be Done?

The nuclear tests in South Asia heightened tensions, raised the prospect of an accelerated arms race and risked deepening the region's chronic poverty by reducing investor confidence, increasing defence expenditure and slowing economic growth. India's claim to greater international status and leadership was weakened, relations with China were aggravated, and internal political stability, especially in Pakistan, was put at risk. Nor did claims to nuclear-weapon status diminish the risks of conflict. The argument, popular in India, that nuclear weapons would never actually be used is untestable until it breaks down, and does not in any case seem to be shared by Pakistan. Islamabad's readiness to support infiltrators in Kashmir just a year after the tests revealed that it did not appreciate how the situation had changed. There can be no certainty that, in some future conflict, there will be no nuclear first-use in response to conventional attack. Although the possibility should not be exaggerated, it is dangerous to rely on an assumption that nuclear weapons will never be used in South Asia.

The nuclear tests also affected arms-control and non-proliferation regimes. Although progress in these areas is difficult for reasons that go beyond South Asia, the tests may make other states feel less constrained in pursuing their own programmes. Pakistan's actions may impinge on Iran. Tehran is already concerned about the influence of the *Taleban* in neighbouring Afghanistan, which receives at least moral support from Islamabad. Military developments in India could affect China, and hence the wider region.

Both India and, to a lesser extent, Pakistan have recognised that international concerns are legitimate, allowing political and military dialogue to take place. These discussions, unprecedented in their intensity, are welcome. India and Pakistan intend to engage constructively with China and Russia, offering the prospect of improved relations. The Lahore Declaration and its accompanying Memorandum of Understanding set out an important work programme for bilateral relations, suggesting that their authors at least were aware of the problems, and determined to tackle them. But the legacy of 50 years of acrimony between India and Pakistan, along with India's long-standing rivalry with China, will not be easily erased. Tangible progress over the underlying problems remains a distant prospect. There is little appetite outside the region for grappling with the Kashmir problem. Indian sensitivity over any third-party engagement, coupled with Pakistan's attempts to secure an exclusive focus on Kashmir, has limited the scope for constructive discussion about wider aspects of South Asian stability, such as trade, the environment, terrorism, drug-trafficking and poverty. The nuclear issue adds a new dimension to these problems. Outside coercion has had little effect, and inducements risk being seen to legitimise unwelcome actions. All the parties concerned will need to face some hard choices if the risks of conflict are to be reduced, and the benchmarks set out by the international community in June 1998 met.

> *the legacy of 50 years of acrimony between India and Pakistan will not be easily erased*

Broad Principles

The priority is to avert war between the region's nuclear-capable countries. Maintaining that conflict will never happen is not credible. Political stability should be encouraged within India and Pakistan, in their relations with each other, and in the wider region. A mechanism for regular discussion going beyond the subcontinent is urgently needed. This might include South-east Asia, Central Asia, China and others. Collective dialogue might be initiated between states that are party to the NPT, and those that are not. Neither the nuclear tests nor Kashmir need be the main emphasis.

China's role is crucial. The suspicion that Chinese entities, possibly acting without government authority, are contravening the NPT and the MTCR undermines international agreements and makes it more difficult to secure Indian adherence to them. (China, although not a member of the MTCR, has publicly agreed to abide by its guidelines.) Progress in resolving border disputes could become disproportionately valuable if it reassured New Delhi about China's strategic intentions and reduced India's perceived need for strategic defences.

Arms control and measures to increase confidence and security also need to be re-examined, adapted and reinforced so as not to erode what has already been achieved. This should be done by building on consensus where it exists, or where it can be secured. International agreements cannot simply be imposed on a sovereign state against its will. Nonetheless, it would be useful to emphasise again that the world is moving in the opposite direction to that chosen by India and Pakistan; and that their tests have made more difficult the ultimate achievement of the nuclear disarmament to which the NPT looks forward, just after a decade of reductions in warhead numbers following the end of the Cold War. Of course, there are still expectations that the NPT-defined nuclear-weapon states should reduce their stocks further. If they fail to do so, they will find it more difficult to impress upon others the importance of arms control and non-proliferation. As long as some nuclear-weapon states fail to ratify the CTBT, and progress over talks on strategic arms reductions is not made, their moral authority and ability to influence debate are diminished.

Specific Actions and Objectives
Nuclear Doctrines

Both India and Pakistan appear to have neglected issues of doctrine. Since nuclear policy will always contain elements that governments will wish to keep secret, it is unclear what either government has done, or intends to do. The main elements needing attention would include:

- refraining from military procurement and deployment which increases rather than diminishes the risk of nuclear conflict;
- steps to make nuclear weapons safe from accidental

detonation and unauthorised interference;

- measures to ensure adequate central or political control of nuclear policy and related activities; and
- procedures to manage the consequences of a nuclear-related political or military incident.

India and Pakistan could also consider the following specific steps:

- explicitly ruling out 'launch-on-warning' policies;
- engaging in operational arms control, including keeping nuclear forces off alert, not attaching warheads and other vital components to delivery systems and extending the time required to make nuclear forces ready for launch; and
- refraining from deploying nuclear-delivery systems.

Building Confidence and Security

The past failure fundamentally to improve relations between India and Pakistan should not deter future efforts to do so. The two countries need to resume their dialogue, using as a starting-point the Memorandum of Understanding accompanying the Lahore Declaration, which neither side has repudiated. For any dialogue to be fruitful, the situation in Kashmir needs to be calm, with no action along the Line of Control. If both governments could then engage in negotiations on all issues of difference between them, they may be able progressively to pull back their security forces at the Line, and to reduce the activities of those that remain.

India may regard itself as the wronged party following the Kargil confrontation in 1999. But this should not mask the fact that the Indian authorities as well as militants and terrorists have violated human rights and alienated many people in the Kashmir Valley and elsewhere. India should recognise that greater access by human-rights observers to the Valley, and increased cooperation with them, could help to limit such violations. New Delhi might also modify its long-standing opposition to UN involvement in the Kashmir issue, at least to the extent of allowing the deployment of UN observers in the Valley, with a larger role for the UN Military Observer Group in India and Pakistan (UNMOGIP). The existing restrictions on UNMOGIP's movements limit its potential value in deterring and moderating low-intensity conflict. Greater autonomy for Jammu and Kashmir, although politically controversial in India, could encourage increased electoral participation by the Valley's people. New Delhi could also take further steps to ensure that its considerable subventions to Jammu and Kashmir reach their intended destinations.

As long as militant activity in the Valley receives support from across the Line of Control, the scope for developing mutual confidence will be severely limited. Pakistan should cease its political and strategic support of armed incursions across the Line, ensure that no official authorities support militants or terrorists, dismantle training camps on Pakistani soil and prevent militant or terrorist groups from using Pakistani territory for training purposes.

Given India's concerns about many aspects of its relations with China, there is an urgent need for progress in bilateral discussion over reducing mutual strategic threats, and for progress in resolving border disputes. In addition, Beijing should ensure that all of China's institutions cease any cooperation with Pakistan's missile and nuclear programmes.

More widely, there is no mechanism for the discussion or elaboration of an 'Asian security architecture', nor is there a forum where regional issues beyond bilateral differences can be aired. The ARF, which seems to have had some effect on relations between ASEAN and China, includes India, but not Pakistan. Bringing Islamabad into the group could be beneficial. However, partly out of reluctance to import the Kashmir issue into ASEAN councils, members have proved unwilling to do so. The Task Force that emerged from the foreign ministers' meeting of June 1998 might be expanded to include representatives from India and Pakistan, while Russia's suggestion in April 1999 for four-way discussions with China, India and Pakistan could also merit further examination.

Arms Control

While progress over arms control in South Asia will be conditioned by progress in international negotiations, international consensus is not necessarily a prerequisite, nor must one country's actions be linked to the other's. Unilateral Indian moves could, for instance, sit well with its refusal to allow third-party involvement in resolving its differences with Pakistan. Islamabad and New Delhi could sign the CTBT independently of each other. The international standing of both countries would also be improved if they agreed to a moratorium on the production of fissile material for nuclear weapons, participated fully in negotiations over fissile materials and worked towards the early signature of a fissile-material treaty. Even if India and Pakistan do not renounce their nuclear weapons and become non-nuclear weapon state parties to the NPT, they could nonetheless conform to the obligations that the treaty places on its nuclear-weapon state parties. Both could also become more closely associated with the NSG and the MTCR, and give more substance to commitments not to export missile or nuclear technology.

In their approach to arms control, outside powers need to take more account of South Asia's particular circumstances. Foreign governments should recognise that regional stability could be increased if states outside the region adhered to arms-control instruments such as the CTBT. Both the NPT and UN Security Council Resolution 1172 preclude recognising either India or Pakistan as nuclear-weapon states. This may not, however, prevent discussion of issues relating to nuclear stability. The extent of the issues that could be discussed without violating the NPT should be carefully examined. The scope of possible assistance in areas such as civil nuclear safety could also be explored. Countries outside the region need to maintain a common approach if they are to encourage progress.

Taken together, these ideas constitute an ambitious and wide-ranging approach. Some, such as nuclear safety and measures to enhance stability, are more urgent than others. But none can be neglected. The process needs to be conducted away from the glare of publicity that has so frequently surrounded South Asian nuclear issues in the past. More than simply bilateral contacts are needed, effective though these can be. To be persuasive, outside actors should develop a deeper understanding of the regional issues, as well as of the domestic circumstances in which both Indian and Pakistani decision-makers operate. Arms-control and regional experts need to cooperate more closely to devise arms-control strategies that work in South Asia. In this way, the outside world may be better able to help India and Pakistan to manage their differences. For India and Pakistan themselves, with their volatile domestic politics, the most important quality will be restraint.

Confidence- and Security-Building Measures

Measures Agreed and Implemented

India and Pakistan have reached agreement on the following confidence- and security-building measures, all of which have, to varying degrees, been implemented:

- neither country will attack the other's nuclear installations;
- neither country will intrude on the other's airspace;
- advance notification of military movements;
- a bilateral agreement 'on the complete prohibition of chemical weapons' (prior to both countries signing the Chemical Weapons Convention, which entered into force in April 1997);
- a code of conduct governing the treatment of diplomats;
- a hotline and staff meetings between headquarters along the Line of Control; and
- a hotline between prime ministers (not used in May 1998).

One-off Gestures

The following are one-off gestures, most of which remain to be implemented or fully developed:

- the opening of a cross-border bus route;
- the release of fishermen held by each side;
- the repatriation of civilian prisoners;
- the easing of travel restrictions;
- increased cultural exchanges;

- greater bilateral trade;
- the Indian purchase of Pakistani electricity;
- collaboration in a gas pipeline from Iran via Pakistan to India; and
- collaboration in flood management.

Measures Discussed

The following measures have been discussed, but have not been agreed:

- the revival of the Indo-Pakistani Joint Commission, a forum for the discussion of a wide range of issues;
- a package of measures *vis-à-vis* the Line of Control, such as improving the implementation of existing agreements, achieving 'compatible' troop levels and cooperating in the promotion of 'peaceful and harmonious relations';
- expanding the coverage of the existing agreement prohibiting attacks on each other's nuclear installations;
- a nuclear no-first-use agreement;
- convening an international conference on peace and security in South Asia; and
- resolving the Siachen Glacier conflict, the Wullar Barrage/ Tulbul Navigation Project water dispute and the Sir Creek boundary dispute.

Other Measures

Other confidence- and security-building measures could also be discussed. These include:

- amending UNMOGIP's mandate to allow its greater involvement in monitoring the Line of Control;
- allowing increased access to the Kashmir Valley by non-governmental organisations concerned with human rights;
- increasing the autonomy and economic development of Jammu and Kashmir;
- an end to incursions by both sides across the Line of Control;
- agreement not to mount nuclear warheads on missiles or to deploy missiles, and measures to verify compliance;

- restrictions on equipment and force sizes in forward areas; and
- ending official support for terrorist or unofficial counter-terrorist organisations.

notes

Acknowledgements

The author would like to thank the many people in the UK, India, Pakistan and elsewhere, who have contributed to this study. The author is particularly grateful to the late Gerald Segal for his advice and support.

Chapter 1

[1] Sumit Ganguly, 'India's Pathway to Pokhran II', *International Security*, vol. 23, no. 4, Spring 1999, p. 158.
[2] Varun Sahni, 'Going Nuclear: Establishing an Overt Weapons Capability', in David Cortright and Amitabh Mattoo (eds), *India and the Bomb* (Notre Dame, IN: University of Notre Dame Press, 1996), p. 89.
[3] Richard A. Best, Jr., *US Intelligence and India's Nuclear Tests: Lessons Learned*, CRS Report for Congress 98-672F (Washington DC: Congressional Research Service (CRS), August 1998).
[4] Bharat Karnad, 'Going Thermonuclear: Why, With What Forces, At What Cost', *Journal of the United Service Institution of India*, vol. 128, no. 53, July–September 1998, p. 310.
[5] William Walker, 'International Nuclear Relations after the Indian and Pakistani Test Explosions', *International Affairs*, vol. 74, no. 3, p. 512.
[6] 'Suo Motu Statement by Prime Minister Shri Atal Bihari Vajpayee in Parliament on 27th May, 1998', Ministry of External Affairs, www.meadev.gov.in/govt/statement-parliament.htm.
[7] The events surrounding these two incidents are described in Devin T. Hagerty, *The Consequences of Nuclear Proliferation* (Cambridge, MA: The MIT Press, 1998).
[8] *Ibid*. See also Scott D. Sagan and Kenneth N. Waltz, *The Spread of Nuclear Weapons: A Debate* (New York: W. W. Norton, 1995).
[9] 'China Is Threat No. 1, Says Fernandes', *Hindustan Times*, 4 May 1998.
[10] N. C. Menon, 'Skewed Logic of Think Tank on Proliferation', *ibid.*, 23 May 1999; and Swaran Singh,

'China's Nuclear Weapons and Doctrine', in Jasjit Singh (ed.), *Nuclear India* (New Delhi: Knowledge World, 1998), pp. 151, 154.

[11] Shirley A. Kan, *Chinese Proliferation of Weapons of Mass Destruction: Background and Analysis*, CRS Report for Congress 96-767F (Washington DC: CRS, September 1996); and Shirley A. Kan, *Chinese Proliferation of Weapons of Mass Destruction: Current Policy Issues*, CRS Issue Brief 92056, (Washington DC: CRS, March 1999).

[12] Kan, *Chinese Proliferation of Weapons of Mass Destruction: Background and Analysis*, pp. 18, 25.

[13] Kan, *Chinese Proliferation of Weapons of Mass Destruction: Current Policy Issues*, pp. 3, 4.

[14] Menon, 'Skewed Logic'.

[15] 'China Is Threat No. 1'.

[16] Raj Chengappa and Manoj Joshi, 'Hawkish India', *India Today*, 1 June 1998.

[17] See N. Ram, 'What Wrong Did This Man Do?', *Frontline*, 8–21 May 1999.

[18] Ganguly, 'India's Pathway to Pokhran II', p. 153.

[19] A. G. Noorani, 'India's Quest for a Nuclear Guarantee', *Asian Survey*, vol. 7, no. 7, July 1967, pp. 490–502.

[20] Morrice James, *Pakistan Chronicle* (London: Hurst, 1993), p. 185.

[21] K. Subrahmanyam, 'Indian Nuclear Policy 1964–98', in Singh (ed.), *Nuclear India*, pp. 39–44.

[22] For details of Indian, Pakistani and Chinese missiles, see Waheguru Pal Singh Sidhu, *Enhancing Indo-US Strategic Cooperation*, Adelphi Paper 313 (Oxford: Oxford University Press for the IISS, 1997), p. 17. For details of missile tests after May 1998, see Andrew Koch, 'South Asian Rivals Keep Test Score Even', *Jane's Intelligence Review*, August 1999, pp. 34–37.

[23] Hilary Synnott, 'The Second Asia–Europe Summit and the ASEM Process', *Asian Affairs*, vol. 30, part 1, February 1999, p. 7.

[24] See, for instance, Karnad, 'Going Thermonuclear', p. 310.

[25] Giri Deshingkar, 'Indian Politics and Arms Control', in Eric Arnett (ed.), *Nuclear Weapons and Arms Control in South Asia after the Test Ban* (Oxford: Oxford University Press for the Stockholm International Peace Research Institute (SIPRI), 1998), pp. 26–29.

[26] Conference on Disarmament Document CD/PV.740, 20 June 1996, p. 16.

[27] Rajesh Rajagopalan, 'Prospects for Peace in South Asia', *The Hindu*, 26 April 1999.

[28] Such an arrangement was reportedly agreed between Indira Gandhi and Zulfikar Ali Bhutto in 1974. See J. N. Dixit, *Anatomy of a Flawed Inheritance* (New Delhi: Konark Publishers, 1995), p. 326.

[29] See, for instance, Hasan-Askari Rizvi, 'Pakistan in 1998: The Polity under Pressure', *Asian Survey*, vol. 39, no. 1, January–February 1999, pp. 177–85.

[30] The Pressler Amendment (Section 620E(e) of the Foreign Assistance Act of 1961) became law in 1985. It requires the US president to certify that Pakistan does not possess a nuclear device during the fiscal year for which US aid is to be provided.

[31] This concern seems to have been groundless: the report was swiftly denied by Israel and India, and no corroboration has been forthcoming. Statement to the Conference on Disarmament by Ambassador Munir Akram, 28 May 1998, www.gn.apc.org/acronym/sppak2.htm.

[32] Munir Ahmad Khan, *Nuclearisation of South Asia and Its Regional and Global Implications* (Islamabad: Institute of Regional Studies, 1998), pp. 8–11.

[33] Aid was suspended under the Symington Amendment to Section 669 of the Foreign Assistance Act. The amendment, passed by the US Congress in 1976, was not retroactive, and so did not apply to India, which had built unsafeguarded reprocessing facilities before it came into effect.

Chapter 2

[1] Philippines Foreign Minister Domingo Lim Siazon, who was ASEAN Regional Forum (ARF) chair at the time, described the issue as the meeting's most contentious. The Indian press, drawing on official Indian briefings, strangely described the ARF's criticism as 'mild'. See, for instance, Manoj Joshi, 'Manila Serenade', *India Today*, 10 August 1998.

[2] Remarkably, the lengthy review and analysis of the international situation in the Non-Aligned Movement (NAM)'s ministerial-level communiqué of 19–20 May 1998 – a week after India's tests – contained no reference to the tests, or to the situation in South Asia.

[3] The Glenn Amendment to Section 102(b) of the Arms Export Control Act of 1976 prohibits US foreign assistance to any non-nuclear-weapon state that detonates a nuclear explosive device. It makes no provision for the lifting of sanctions once they are imposed.

[4] William J. Long, 'Non-proliferation as a Goal of Japanese Foreign Assistance', *Asian Survey*, vol. 39, no. 2, March–April 1999, pp. 338–41.

[5] Russia's decision to help build a nuclear power station in India caused particular dismay in the West, where the move was seen as a breach of the guidelines of the Nuclear Suppliers' Group (NSG). Moscow maintained that its agreement with India was permissible because it followed on from a contract which predated the NSG's requirement for full-scope safeguards.

[6] See, for example, Sahni, 'Going Nuclear', in Cortright and Mattoo (eds), *India and the Bomb*, p. 96.

[7] Barbara Leitch LePoer (coordinator), *India–Pakistan Nuclear Tests and US Response*, CRS Report for Congress 98-570F (Washington DC: CRS, November 1998).

[8] Strobe Talbott, 'US Diplomacy in South Asia: A Progress Report', speech given at the Brookings Institution, Washington DC, 12 November 1998; and Strobe Talbott, 'Dealing with the Bomb in South Asia', *Foreign Affairs*, vol. 78, no. 2, March–April 1999, p. 120.

[9] Press Trust of India (PTI), 'Chinese Cool to Russia's Quadrangle Proposal', *Hindustan Times*, 24 April 1999.

[10] See, for example, V. R. Raghavan, 'China, India and Kashmir', *The Hindu*, 15 June 1999.

[11] C. Raja Mohan, 'India for Closer Ties with US, China', *ibid.*, 25 July 1999.

[12] Jaswant Singh, *Defending India* (New York: St. Martin's Press, 1999), p. 186.

[13] K. K. Katyal, 'Undo Aggression, PM Tells Pak', *The Hindu*, 8 June 1999; and Adrian Levy and Sumit Das Gupta, 'Nuclear Alert Sounded in Pakistan', *The Sunday Times*, 30 May 1999.

[14] 'Kashmir Fighters Will Be Asked

to Redeploy, Pakistan Army Chief
Says', *International Herald Tribune*, 7
July 1999.
[15] Pamela Constable, 'Border
Conflict Ebbs as Fighters Leave
Kashmir', *Washington Post*, 17 July
1999.
[16] 'Pakistan Army Holds Key Peaks
on Kashmir Border: Spokesman',
Dawn, 26 July 1999.
[17] John Lancaster, 'Kashmir Crisis
Was Defused on Brink of War',
Washington Post, 26 July 1999.
[18] Press Release, Indian Ministry of
External Affairs, 27 July 1999,
www.meadev.gov.in/news/
official/19990727/official.htm.
[19] 'PM Got First-ever US
Comittment on Kashmir:
Mushahid', *Dawn*, 25 July 1999.
[20] Thomas W. Lippman, 'India
Hinted at Attack in Pakistan',
Washington Post, 27 June 1999.
[21] Amy Louise Kazmin, 'Pakistan
Admits Kashmir Incursions',
Financial Times, 17 July 1999.
[22] *Asian Age*, 21 July 1999.

Chapter 3

[1] Jaswant Singh, *Defending India*,
p. 333.
[2] Dilip Lahiri, *Formalising Restraint:
The Case of South Asia*, paper
presented at the Ninth
International Arms Control
Conference, Albuquerque, NM, 17
April 1999, www.meadev.gov.in/
govt/sp-undc1704.htm.
[3] Article I of the Nuclear Non-
Proliferation Treaty (NPT) requires
'Each nuclear-weapon State Party
to the Treaty … not in any way to
assist, encourage, or induce any
non-nuclear-weapon State Party to
manufacture or otherwise acquire
nuclear weapons or other nuclear
explosive devices, or control over
such weapons or explosive

devices.' The NPT does not offer
any exceptions to this rule.
[4] Michael Joseph Wilmshurst,
'Reforming the Non-proliferation
System in the 1980s', in John
Simpson and Anthony G. McGrew
(eds), *The International Nuclear Non-
proliferation System: Challenges and
Choices* (London: Macmillan, 1984),
pp. 145–49.
[5] Walker, 'International Nuclear
Relations', p. 522; Michael Quinlan,
'Nuclear Tests in the Subcontinent:
Prospects and Significance for the
World', *International Relations*, vol.
14, no. 4, April 1999, pp. 4–5.
[6] See, for example, M. V. Ramana,
'Disturbing Issues', *Frontline*, 22
May–4 June 1999.
[7] Jacques Chirac, Tony Blair and
Gerhard Schröder, 'The Test Ban
Treaty Needs American
Ratification', *International Herald
Tribune*, 9 October 1999.
[8] Karnad, 'Going Thermonuclear',
p. 312.
[9] 'Announcement on Television by
Foreign Minister Gohar Ayub
Khan, 30 May 1998',
news2.this.bbc.co.uk/olmedia/
100000/audio/
_103193_gohar_ayub_khan_.ram.
[10] *Times of India*, 24 April 1999.
[11] 'No Transfer of Nuclear
Technology', *Dawn*, 20 May 1999.
[12] 'Ties with Pakistan to Grow, Says
General Chi', *Dawn*, 23 February
1999.
[13] Michael Newbill, 'English Media
Commentary in India and Pakistan
on Confidence-Building Measures,
1990–97', in Michael Krepon (ed.),
*A Handbook of CBMs for Regional
Security* (Washington DC: Henry L
Stimson Center, 1998), p. 1.
[14] *Times of India*, 28 April 1998.
[15] C. Raja Mohan criticises this
tendency to 'internationalise' the
Kashmir issue, which emerged
even before the successful

agreement on a withdrawal. See 'India and the US after Kargil', *The Hindu*, 24 June 1999; and 'PM Got First-ever US Commitment on Kashmir'.

[16] Sartaj Aziz, quoted in 'Pakistan Slams Delhi's Hegemonistic Policies', *Dawn*, 24 September 1999.

Chapter 4

[1] Michael Quinlan, *Thinking about Nuclear Weapons*, RUSI Whitehall Paper 41 (London: Royal United Services Institution (RUSI), 1997), p. 8.

[2] Jaswant Singh, *Defending India*, p. 336.

[3] Michael Quinlan defines deterrence as 'inducing someone to refrain from unwanted action by putting before him the prospect that taking it will prompt a response with disadvantages to him outweighing the advantages of the action'. Quinlan, *Thinking about Nuclear Weapons*, p. 12.

[4] Geoffrey Kemp has identified five basic requirements for all nuclear forces: survivability; reliability; command, control and communications; penetration; and target identification, destruction and mission assessment. Geoffrey Kemp, *Nuclear Forces for Medium Powers, Part 1*, Adelphi Paper 107 (London: IISS, 1974), p. 19. See also Clayton P. Bowen and Daniel Wolven, 'Command and Control Challenges in South Asia', *Nonproliferation Review*, vol. 6, no. 3, Spring/Summer 1999, pp. 25–35.

[5] Joint Statement by the DEA and DRDO, www.meadev.gov.in/govt/drdo.htm.

[6] David Albright, 'Shots Heard 'Round the World', *Bulletin of the Atomic Scientists*, July–August 1998, pp. 21–23; 'We Have an Adequate Scientific Database for Designing a Credible Nuclear Deterrent', interview with R. Chidambaram, *Frontline*, 2 January 1999. In late 1998, S. K. Sikka of India's Bhabha Atomic Research Centre (BARC) was quoted as claiming that a boosted-fission device was used in the first stage. Raj Chengappa, 'Is India's H-Bomb a Dud?', *India Today*, 12 October 1998.

[7] 'After the Tests: India and Pakistan Update', *Bulletin of the Atomic Scientists*, vol. 54, no. 5, September–October 1998; and Debra Mackenzie, 'Making Waves', *New Scientist*, 13 June 1998.

[8] Mark Hibbs, 'India Test Questioned', *Nucleonics Weekly*, 10 June 1999, p. 13.

[9] David Albright, Frans Berkhout and William Walker, *Plutonium and Highly Enriched Uranium 1996: World Inventories, Capabilities and Policies* (New York: Oxford University Press, 1997), p. 269, quoted in Rodney W. James and Mark G. McDonough, *Tracking Nuclear Proliferation, 1998: India* (Washington DC: Carnegie Endowment for International Peace, 1998), pp. 111, 112.

[10] See Robert S. Norris and William N. Arkin, 'After the Tests: India and Pakistan Update', *NRDC Nuclear Notebook*, vol. 54, no. 5, September–October 1998; and Barbara Leitch LePoer, *India–US Relations*, CRS Issue Brief IB93097 (Washington DC: CRS, 27 April 1999), p. 5.

[11] Waheguru Pal Singh Sidhu, 'Building a Nuclear Triad and Second Strike Capability', paper presented at the conference 'Nuclearisation of South Asia', Como, Italy, May 1999, www.ceip.org/programs/npp/sidhu3.htm; and Ian Steer, 'Asia's Rival Reactors a Cause for Concern', *Jane's Intelligence Review*,

October 1998, p. 26.

[12] Anwar Iqbal, 'How Did They Pay for It? Not through BCCI, Honest, Says Pakistan's Dr Strangelove', *The Observer*, 31 May 1998.

[13] François Heisbourg, 'The Prospects for Nuclear Stability between India and Pakistan', *Survival*, vol. 40, no. 4, Winter 1998–99, p. 79.

[14] Leitch LePoer, *India–US Relations*, p. 5; and Norris and Arkin, 'After the Tests'.

[15] See Steer, 'Asia's Rival Reactors'.

[16] See Brahma Chellaney, 'After the Tests: India's Options', *Survival*, vol. 40, no. 4, Winter 1998–99, p. 106.

[17] See 'Reactions to India's Nuclear Tests of May 1998: Archives', www.meadev.gov.in/govt/offl_stm.htm.

[18] Rahul Bedi, 'Interview: George Fernandes, Indian Defence Minister', *Jane's Defence Weekly*, 1 July 1998, p. 32.

[19] 'Atal Constitutes Six-Member National Security Council', *Hindustan Times*, 20 November 1998; 'A National Security Council at Last', *The Hindu*, 21 November 1998.

[20] 'Draft Report of National Security Advisory Board on Indian Nuclear Doctrine', 17 August 1999, www.mea.gov.in/govt/indnucld.htm; and 'Create Credible N-Arsenal', *The Hindu*, 18 August 1999.

[21] The sensitivities lying behind such allegations are powerful and probably widely felt. See, for example, K. Sundarji, 'India's Nuclear Weapons Policy', in Jorn Gjelstad and Olav Nolstad (eds), *Nuclear Rivalry and International Order* (Oslo: International Peace Research Institute, 1996), p. 179.

[22] Address by Prime Minister Nawaz Sharif, 28 May 1998, www.pak.gov.pk.

[23] See, for instance, 'No Change in Pakistan's Nuclear Strategy', *Dawn*, 20 June 1999.

[24] Statement by Ambassador Munir Akram, Plenary Meeting, Conference on Disarmament, Geneva, 14 May 1998, www.gn.apc.org/acronym/sppak.htm.

[25] M. Ziauddin, 'Pakistani Nuclear Doctrine Being Finalised: FM', *Dawn*, 19 August 1999; and Sartaj Aziz, 'India's Nuclear Doctrine: A Pakistani Perspective', www.pak.gov.pk/personal/main/india_doctrine.htm.

[26] For discussions of this issue, see Hagerty, *The Consequences of Nuclear Proliferation*, pp. 39–62, 178; and Jasjit Singh (ed.), *Nuclear India*, pp. 309–11. For a counter-view, see Neil Joeck, *Maintaining Nuclear Stability in South Asia*, Adelphi Paper 312 (Oxford: Oxford University Press for the IISS, 1997), pp. 48–50.

[27] Jasjit Singh, 'A Nuclear Strategy for India', in Jasjit Singh (ed.), *Nuclear India*, p. 310.

[28] Lawrence Freedman, *The Evolution of Nuclear Strategy* (London: Macmillan for the IISS, 1989), p. 207.

[29] Singh, 'A Nuclear Strategy for India', pp. 309–15.

[30] K. Subrahmanyam, 'Nuclear Force Design and Minimum Deterrence Strategy for India', in Cortright and Mattoo (eds), *India and the Bomb*, pp. 92–93.

[31] Chellaney, 'After the Tests', p. 107.

[32] Singh (ed.), *Nuclear India*, pp. 170–72.

[33] Karnad, 'Going Thermonuclear', p. 314. According to the Carnegie Endowment for International Peace (CEIP), China has some 400 nuclear warheads, France 450 and the UK 192. CEIP, 'Nuclear Numbers', www.ceip.org/programs/npp/

numbers/numbers.htm.

[34] *Frontline* magazine in India and the development of New Social Movements in Pakistan are notable examples of such opposition.

[35] Vijai Nair, 'National Security: Strategic Command and Control Structures', *Journal of the United Service Institution of India*, vol. 128, no. 533, July–September 1998, pp. 348, 359.

[36] Bruce G. Blair, *The Logic of Accidental Nuclear War* (Washington DC: The Brookings Institution, 1993), pp. 169, 173.

[37] Levy and Gupta, 'Nuclear Alert Sounded in Pakistan'.

[38] Eric Arnett, 'Conventional Arms Transfers and Nuclear Stability in South Asia', in Arnett (ed.), *Nuclear Weapons and Arms Control in South Asia*, pp. 84–88.

[39] Singh, 'A Nuclear Strategy for India', p. 317.

[40] Kapil Kak, 'Command and Control of Small Nuclear Arsenals',

in Singh (ed.), *Nuclear India*, pp. 270–71.

[41] 'Pakistan Should Respond, Says COAS', *Dawn*, 13 April 1999.

[42] Paul Bracken, *The Command and Control of Nuclear Forces* (New Haven, CT: Yale University Press, 1983), p. 228.

[43] Kan, *Chinese Proliferation of Weapons of Mass Destruction: Current Policy Issues*, pp. 3, 5.

[44] Karnad, 'Going Thermonuclear'. For a more realistic view, see Waheguru Pal Singh Sidhu, 'A Sea-Based Deterrent', *The Hindu*, 22 May 1999.

[45] Stephen I. Schwartz (ed.), *Atomic Audit: The Costs and Consequences of US Nuclear Weapons Since 1940* (Washington DC: Brookings Institution, 1998), www.brook.edu/press/books/atomic.htm.

[46] *Deterrence, Arms Control and Proliferation: Strategic Defence Review* (London: The Stationery Office, 1998), pp. 5–8.